Toughing It Out

ADVENTURES OF A GLOBAL ENTREPRENEUR

John Holliday

TALLAI BOOKS
Gold Coast, Australia

Copyright © 2012 by John Holliday.

All rights reserved. No part of this publication may be reproduced, distributed or transmitted in any form or by any means, including photocopying, recording, or other electronic or mechanical methods, without the prior written permission of the publisher, except in the case of brief quotations embodied in critical reviews and certain other noncommercial uses permitted by copyright law. For permission requests, write to the publisher at the address below.

Tallai Books
5 Earle Court
Tallai, Qld 4213, Australia
www.tallaibooks.com

Book Layout ©2015 BookDesignTemplates.com

Toughing It Out: Adventures of a Global Entrepreneur.

Paperback: ISBN 9780648684831

eBook: ISBN 9780648684824

CONTENTS

FEDERAL COURT OF AUSTRALIA 7
BEGINNINGS 17
CHANGING UNIFORMS 27
CONTINENTAL SHIFT. 31
BREAKING OUT 39
OPEN TO CHANGE. 47
BALANCING ACT 55
ON MY OWN 61
NETWORKING 69
PRIVATE LIFE UPHEAVALS 81
SHIFTING BUSINESS GEARS 89
OPTIONS GALORE 97
CHANGING CONTINENTS. 105
RAISING THE ODDS. 119
ACROSS AUSTRALIA'S OUTBACK. 127
THE BIRTH OF ORION 137
ORION'S DOG COLLAR. 147
GOING SOLAR. 163

GIVING BACK 169

AIMING TO BE THE BEST 175

THREAT MEETS OPPORTUNITY 179

END GAME. 189

LOOKING BACK 195

NO SUNSETS 205

About the Author. 211

FOREWORD

THIS BOOK HAS STARTED as a personal endeavour to recall some of the rewarding and interesting experiences from my business life and to present a chronicle of the characters that I have worked with over the years. The whole venture was intended to be primarily for my own benefit or maybe for family members present and future.

As the journal progressed I started to think that this could also be of interest to anyone who has an interest in or is actively developing a business for themselves. I often read how famous entrepreneurs build companies and the bookshelves are full of volumes about the Richard Bransons, Steve Jobs and Henry Fords of this world. As fascinating as the lives of these big time achievers are, their stories have little in common with the millions of small time entrepreneurs that might find an interest in my story. I think that every one of my business ventures has lessons for anyone starting or building a small or medium business. The challenge for me is to record those lessons and ideas in a way that is interesting to the reader.

I have documented stories from nine businesses which I have built with varying degrees of success throughout my career and I have made mention of other business ideas which failed to get off the ground for whatever reason. Out of this assortment of business exploits a potential entrepreneur is sure to pick up some idea of what or what not to do.

I have also included tales of some of the wonderful characters that I have worked with over the years, because they have really added to the fun of it all. To anyone that I worked with through the adventure of building those companies, thank you. You added to my experience and to my ultimate success. All of the companies leading up to the last one were for practice only and your participation was an essential ingredient which made the practice worthwhile.

Finally I have put together some thoughts about what motivated me and what makes an entrepreneur generally. I hope that you will find it interesting.

CHAPTER 1

FEDERAL COURT OF AUSTRALIA

IT IS OCTOBER, 2001 and Justice Mark Weinberg addresses the two opposing legal teams, announcing the adjournment for the day and asking us to resume at 10 o'clock the following morning.

"What an enormous relief!" I tell myself. I am in Melbourne, in the Federal Court of Australia. Having been cross-examined on the witness stand all day, I had undergone a brutally tough grilling by the Queen's Counsel of the Respondent.

The black-gowned QCs, barristers, court officials and people occupying the public gallery rise and bow as the judge leaves the court room. The noise of conversations breaking out, and feet shuffling as people begin to leave, contrast sharply against a day where only one person at a time had spoken.

Soul depleted, body exhausted, I quiz our legal team to find out how I had performed under cross-examination. Their verdict: I didn't do badly, but if our lawyers had been on the other side, I would have been crucified. This isn't quite what I want to hear. As I leave the courtroom, I am told that, under no circumstances, am I to discuss what went on in court today. My wife, Colleen, would be taking the stand right after me, tomorrow, and the opposing legal team would try to determine if we had colluded over our testimony.

Colleen and I were staying at a hotel in Melbourne for the duration of the court hearings, so it was going to be a difficult eighteen hours of lips zipped shut. She greeted me at the door of our room with an excited, "How did you go?"

"Sorry;" I pleaded, "Can't say a word." We went to a movie to take our minds off the case but I can't remember what film we saw. Afterwards, we went for dinner, all the while avoiding the topic of the day's events.

This court case was an action we had initiated, some eighteen months earlier, in an attempt to protect our company and ourselves from an unfair campaign of misinformation being whipped up in the popular media by the Royal Society for the Prevention of Cruelty to Animals (RSPCA). Our company was Innotek Australia, and the product we were selling and promoting was an electronic containment system for dogs. The system used an electronic collar which would activate a static pulse to the dog if it attempted to cross a radio field, set up around the perimeter of the containment premises. In effect, it discouraged a dog from escaping from its owner's property and it did so in a fairly gentle way. Our company was being portrayed in the newspapers and on TV news and current affairs programs as a purveyor of products which were cruel to dogs. No evidence was offered to support the allegations; just lots of emotional reference to electric shocks and torture. No matter what we tried, we could not get our side of the story across to the public. Unless we did something, we would be put out of business. Since Colleen and I had everything we owned tied up in the business, this would have meant bankruptcy. I had solicited advice from various sources to combat the campaign aimed against us, but without success. I spoke with a professor of public relations at Bond University, in Queensland. After hearing our predicament, his response was, "Oh, I'm sorry. There's nothing you can do against an organisation like the RSPCA."

Our lawyer, Paul Everingham, felt our only option was to take action in the courts against those parties spreading the false information. He warned us that it could be a very long and tough fight and there was no guarantee we would win. We weighed our options and decided that we would have to fight back.

Our case was originally launched in the Federal Court, in Brisbane, against The Courier Mail newspaper, the Melbourne Herald Sun, RSPCA Victoria, and the RSPCA President, Dr. Hugh Wirth. The first court hearing was won by the other side which resulted in the legal battle being continued in the Federal Court in Melbourne. Our case against The Courier Mail and the Herald Sun disintegrated when the Court accepted their submission that they had reported only what had been reliably reported to them.

The negative publicity about our products continued to grow and if it was not stopped, we would have been out of business before we could get to court. We were now forced to apply to the Court for an injunction, while the case was under review. Although we did not win the injunction, the RSPCA had made it unnecessary by giving a voluntary undertaking not to distribute any more damaging information about us until the matter was settled. When, the very next week, a 200,000-piece direct-mail campaign against us was sent out by the RSPCA, it was put down to an oversight due to having something already in the pipeline.

Painful delays filled the days before the hearing in October. A mediation was held in Melbourne which was unsuccessful. The Mediator could not accept that he was unable to resolve the case and, at one point, chased after us down the street to get us to return for one last try, all to no avail. At times, we felt we would never get to court. But these delays were not wasted by Paul Everingham. He was amassing volumes of evidence and collecting affidavits from customers, suppliers, and anyone else who had some expertise in our products. He arranged for expert witnesses from around the country to attend the hearings and he set up video links for evidence to be presented by experts in the United States, New Zealand and Germany. A court date was set and two weeks allowed for the conduct of the hearing.

This case was costing us dearly, but the longer we survived in business, the greater our chances of being able to meet those costs. In effect, our customers were paying for the legal costs, by way of the higher prices we were charging in Australia for just this reason. Nowhere else in the world did our product have this kind of opposition, so we had factored in this cost when we originally set our pricing. Despite this move, it was still extremely tough for us to meet the soaring legal costs and I am sure the opposing legal team were aware of this. If they could make us run out of money, the case would be dropped and they would have no case to answer. Each day, during the hearings, the opposing QC would rise and ask the judge if he would consider throwing out the case, on the basis that, if we lost, we would not have the funds to pay the other side's costs.

Our legal team countered with a proposal that Colleen and I put up a daily bank guarantee of $25,000 to the Federal Court to cover this eventuality. The judge agreed, but our bank accounts were nearly empty and our house was mortgaged to the hilt. We appealed to our bank for some short-term extension of our credit line. A meeting with the Melbourne branch manager of Citibank was urgently arranged and the bank agreed to go to an absolute maximum of $150,000. This meant that, if the court case went beyond six days, we were finished. So, for four consecutive days, Colleen and I would visit Citibank, sign some documents and provide a further $25,000 guarantee to the Court. For the rest of that week we were on tenterhooks.

On the fifth day, when the opposing QC tried the same case-dismissal argument, the judge responded that Mr. and Mrs. Holliday had put up enough of a guarantee and he would not require us to increase it. Unknown to anyone, we could not have met the demand for additional guarantees and the case would have been lost, there and then. We had just scraped through and perhaps this was an omen.

So here I was, next morning, returning to the Federal Court building on the corner of William and Latrobe Streets to resume our battle for survival. This was surely one of the toughest things I had confronted during my long and varied business career. If we lost this case, it would mean certain bankruptcy. At the age of 59, my chances of starting all over again were rapidly evaporating. Yet, little did I know, that morning, that I would not discover whether we had won or lost our case for another nine months.

The legal team on both sides included a Queen's Counsel (QC), a barrister and a solicitor, plus support staff. The team we assembled were Tony Morris QC, Paul Smith, our barrister, and Paul Everingham and his legal secretary, all of whom had to be flown in from Brisbane and accommodated in a hotel at our cost.

Sometimes, Paul left me wondering why he had called certain witnesses, and not others, but the outcomes always proved that he had done the right thing. One such witness was a Mrs. Barrow, who spoke about her dog, Rupert. She had purchased a containment system for Rupert and she proceeded to tell the Court, in very colourful language, how Rupert would habitually sit close to his boundary with the collar beeping, until the battery went flat, and then he would escape from the property. During one such escape, Rupert was picked up by the RSPCA. When they saw the collar on the dog, Mrs. Barrow was warned not to use the collar again. Now, this same RSPCA inspector who had issued the warning was called to the stand by Paul and questioned why he had not charged Barrow for using the collar.

The inspector replied he could see nothing wrong with the collar, but he had been instructed to stop people from using such a device. This statement clearly refuted the RSPCA's claim that anyone using such a collar would be prosecuted by them.

The final part of Mrs. Barrow's testimony brought tears to many in the court. She told how the RSPCA had ordered her to tie Rupert to a rope. She did as she was told. Arriving home from work, one day, she found that Rupert had jumped the fence and hung himself.

Occasionally, the proceedings would break the courtroom tension. When Dr. Robert Holmes, the noted animal behaviourist, was called to the stand and gave his name and occupation, the judge peered over his glasses and retorted,

"What; are you some kind of dog shrink?"

And when a Brisbane dog trainer showed up in court as one of our witnesses, he looked as though he hadn't changed his clothes for a week. Paul Everingham leaned over to Colleen and asked her to see what she could do to "Clean that guy up, before he takes the stand."

Following my day-long cross-examination on the witness stand the previous day, the worst of my ordeal was behind me. I returned to the stand in the morning and Colleen was called to testify after the lunch recess. She was not required for very long. Now, we could sit in the courtroom and try to analyse what was going on.

Emotions ran high throughout the case, especially when our nemesis, the RSPCA's Dr. Hugh Wirth, took the stand. Our legal team picked at his every response, rationalising why he would respond the way he did. The judge seemed to display no emotion in this regard and took the testimony in a calm, factual manner. Even so, I found it fascinating how the opposing lawyers presented testimony which would arouse emotion in an attempt to sway the judge's opinion. The RSPCA called an elderly veterinarian lady in a wheelchair to describe how an electronic dog collar had burned her forearm. Yet, under cross-examination, it appeared that in her affidavit she had said that it burned her finger. The RSPCA barrister's next witness was a former State Premier who testified what a wonderful person Dr. Hugh Wirth was, but the judge indicated that he did not need any more character witnesses for Dr. Wirth.

A case such as this should be decided on the basis of scientific fact and this is what it came down to, eventually. The RSPCA had called, as an expert witness, an electrical engineer who had analysed an electronic collar and reported the measurements he had taken from the device. This particular collar had been taken off a dog which had suffered pressure necrosis as a result of the collar being worn too long and too tightly. A picture of this dog had been used on the front page of the Herald Sun to show "burn" marks from the electronic collar. In order to support the claims made by the RSPCA in their many interviews with the news media, the RSPCA's barrister questioned the engineer, to confirm the capacity of the collar to generate shocks of 3,000 volts. But during cross-examination, the engineer admitted that the collar was not working at the time it was worn by the dog, thereby disproving the claims of burns. The expert witness had identified a broken connection inside the collar which proved it could not have been functioning at the time. This fact would certainly have been known to the RSPCA, before they ran their anti-collar media campaign.

Tony Morris QC then launched into the electrical engineer and asked him if he knew Ohm's Law. This being a most basic principle of electricity, the engineer snapped, "Of course I know Ohm's Law!" Morris then asked the engineer to estimate the electrical resistance of a dog's skin and the current that the collar was capable of delivering to a dog wearing it. Upon hearing the engineer's answer, Morris asked, "What then, using Ohm's Law, would be the voltage emitted by the collar?" The reply was two volts. Morris eyed the judge and declared, "I have no further questions, Your Honour." The RSPCA's claim of 3,000-volt shocks to a dog now looked decidedly false and misleading.

The RSPCA's expert witness had inadvertently brought this case to a close. The hearing had taken two weeks, brought us enormous stress, and cost us a small entrepreneurial fortune.

Nine months later, the Court handed down it's judgement:

"In my opinion, Innotek has clearly established that at least two of the imputations upon which it relied, were made by the RSPCA. I refer specifically to the statements in the Herald Sun article that the collars inflicted 3,000 volt shocks, and that they had burned dogs' necks. Those imputations were plainly defamatory. On balance, I consider that Innotek has also established that Mr Apostolides told Mr Papps that Innotek had supplied products which had killed a dog (meaning had led directly to the death of the animal, not affected its behaviour so that it ultimately had to be destroyed). These statements were made by Mr Apostolides while acting in the course of his employment, and on behalf of the RSPCA. They were made with full knowledge that they were likely to be reported, and with the intention that that occur. In those circumstances, the RSPCA cannot avoid responsibility for what Mr Apostolides said."

We were awarded damages of $100,000, plus costs, according to a schedule which probably covered 60-70% of our actual costs. In addition, the Court found for the RSPCA, in the cross-claim over the injunction, that we had defamed Dr. Hugh Wirth and it awarded him $25,000. That was an expensive lesson to be very, very careful when dealing with litigation.

Was all this agony worth the fight? Definitely. There was no monetary gain in winning the action, since our costs exceeded what was awarded by the Court, but there was a vindication of our company and its products. The claims that were being made against us had been proven false and, if made again, would probably be declared a contempt of Court. We had silenced our critics and that was worth all the stress and costs of the case because the criticism, if allowed to continue, would have put us out of business.

Is the battle over? I'm afraid not. The powerful animal welfare groups are still campaigning against us, behind the scenes, and their criticism is implied in their opposition to our products. But now they need to campaign against us, based on scientific fact, and this has tilted the playing field in our favour.

We would not have won this case without the legal team that Paul Everingham had put together. His selection of Tony Morris QC to argue our case in Federal Court was exemplary. Tony has an impressive legal career and when he was appointed as Queen's Counsel, at the age of 32, it was the youngest such appointment in Australian legal history and the youngest, in any Commonwealth country, during the twentieth century. He has an impressive assortment of clients, including former Australian Prime Minister, Bob Hawke, Federal and State Ministers, and some of Australia's major corporations.

For anyone confronting a situation even remotely like mine, I have this advice: always go with the best legal advice you can get; do not try to save money on legal fees.

Tony Morris shared a quotation with me which sums up this opening chapter: Where litigation seems inevitable, Igitur qui desiderat pacem, praeparet bellum—therefore, he who wishes for peace, let him make ready for war.

CHAPTER 2

BEGINNINGS

TOUGHING IT OUT: EASY to say, but it requires dealing with the hard things in life. We tend to avoid these, hoping that someone else—perhaps a close friend or associate at work—will do this for us. For a lot of budding entrepreneurs, this anticipation of hardship motivates them to enter into a business partnership because it appears easier if you have someone else to share the burden and confront the tough decisions.

I had always dreamed of running my own business and becoming independently wealthy. But it took me a long time to figure out the secrets of making that dream come true. Even while still at school, I was actively working on business ideas. When I was twelve years old, I bought a gross (12 dozen copies) of the Old Moores Almanac. This book gave forecasts of weather and good fortune and, if I remember correctly, was based on astrology and similar concepts. Today, as a member of Australian Skeptics, I would condemn this publication as a charlatan's comic book. Back then, I had decided that the Old Moores Almanac would be a popular item around the estates of Hemel Hempstead, so with my friend, Collin Brown, I went door to door until they were all sold. Including my friend in this business venture made the exercise psychologically easier for me. I may not have fully appreciated this effect at the time, but I quickly learned that a good business deal was to buy in bulk (at a low price) and sell individually at a much higher price.

I was born during World War II, the second son of parents whose marriage ended in tragedy. Norah Bates was a young dental nurse and, on one summer day in the 1930s, she met George Holliday, a part-time pharmacy student and bicycle mechanic. Living in neighbouring towns in West Hertfordshire, each would trek five or six miles along treed lanes to meet at country pubs in the English countryside. They were a popular young couple living in a place which would soon be torn apart by war. Their idyllic marriage was overshadowed by the diagnosis that George had Hodgkin's disease, a cancer of the lymph nodes, which in those days was untreatable. Their love for each other and the fact that his condition would go into remission, from time to time, gave Norah and George hope that all would turn out well and they could continue building a life together. My brother, Guy, came along in 1939, and I was born in 1942. George's greatest frustration was his rejection from active war service and having to satisfy himself with a role in the Home Guard. He worried about what his boys would think of him upon learning that their father did not fight in the war. His disease worsened and George died on my third birthday, in January, 1945.

Because of his diagnosis, George was unable to get life insurance at a time when there were no social welfare benefits. Since he had not seen active duty in the war, there was no government support available for his widow or his family. But for the stoicism of my mother, I think Guy and I might have been sent to an orphanage or put up for adoption. We moved in with my grandfather and my mother went back to work six days a week. For the next eight years, Norah Holliday had almost no social life and dedicated her time to raising her two boys. At times, I feel guilty about how little I had done for her, compared to all that she had done for me.

Despite all this, I had a very happy childhood. I was a tall, skinny boy and my friends' mothers were always trying to feed me, thinking I didn't get enough food at home. I was too uncoordinated to be good at any sport but I had a wide variety of interests, lots of friends, and my academic achievements were as good as could be expected at the state school I attended. I was aware that we were quite poor but most of my school friends were from London families which had been rehoused because of the war, so they were living under similar circumstances. Possibly as many as fifty of the students were from homes for orphans or children with one parent who had been unable to provide support after the war, a fate my mother worked so hard to avert. I have often wondered what had happened to those children; apparently, many had been shipped to Canada and Australia, leaving behind family members in England.

In stark contrast to our situation were two cousins of mine, at about my age, who were decidedly from the other side of the tracks. Their parents owned their own house, a car and a television set. The boys attended private schools, taking subjects like Latin, which was completely alien to us, and playing sports like rugby, while we played football. We even spoke with different accents. As a result, my brother and I were constantly compared to our cousins and I am sure that this had a profound effect on the person I turned out to be.

But the biggest shaper of my character was my mother's younger brother, Uncle Dick. When we first went to live with my grandfather, Dick was still in the Royal Air Force but his home was our home whenever he was on leave. Dick taught me to ride a bike, built me a toboggan and allowed me to play with his flying gear. He was also the father figure who stood over me when I was required to do the dishes or some other household chore. He was a hero figure to me because he spent the war as a navigator flying RAF Wellington and Halifax bombers over Germany. I know that he completed two tours of duty which I think means flying 50 missions. With his example, he instilled in me the need to study and work hard toward a goal. To be a navigator on a wartime bomber required someone who excelled in mathematics and science and who could operate under extreme pressure. Without those skills and qualities, the air crew would likely not return home from a mission. To me, Uncle Dick was the ultimate quiet achiever.

When I was about thirteen, my mother remarried. My stepfather, Sandy Bailey, owned a second-hand car business, giving me the chance to observe at close hand how a small business was run. It must have been difficult for Sandy to take on the role of a father to two teenage boys, but he did a great job, considering that my brother, Guy, and I were somewhat difficult to control. I used to work at Sandy's car yard during school holidays, cleaning cars and doing odd jobs. I recall being impressed by the size of the business and by the number of seemingly influential people that Sandy knew. Perhaps this had an influence on me, because I've always kept in contact with the people I ran into, throughout my life.

Sandy had served as a major in the Royal Artillery during the war, but spent most of his time as a prisoner of the Japanese, working on the Burma Railway which ran between Bangkok, Thailand and Rangoon, Burma. That's the railway built by the Japanese between 1942 and 1943 and immortalized by the film, "The Bridge on the River Kwai." Forced labour was used to construct the railway and 16,000 Allied prisoners of war died on this project, including 6,318 British personnel. Prisoners were brutally treated by the Japanese soldiers and living and working conditions on the Burma Railway were horrific. Sandy never spoke about that time and, later in life, when I was doing business in Japan, Mum asked me not to speak about Japan while he was present. I know that he had to get special shoes made because of injuries he received while being tortured. I can certainly understand his reluctance to talk about those years of cruel, inhuman treatment. Sandy was very good to my mother and they spent the rest of their lives together until Sandy died in 1990, four years before Mum did.

Like many of my age peers, after finishing school I went to work for an organisation. It was a large insurance company and well known in our community. There, at the London and Lancashire Insurance Company, I could become part of a team, they would teach me how to grow and develop in the business world, and my friends would respect me because some of the respect for the organisation would rub off on me. But this attraction soon faded and I could not discipline myself for the concentration and study required to obtain the qualification of Associate of the Chartered Insurance Institute.

As a junior clerk, I was able to observe the retirement of the loyal wage earner who sat at the end of my Dickensian desk at the company's office in Chancery Lane, London. I forget his name, but his image is with me forever. Picture Bob Cratchett without the limp, complete with the forelock-tugging, head-bowing attitude of the trusted and faithful employee of 50 years and you have it. I had finished school in 1958 so this meant that my ageing colleague had started working in 1908. Apart from his service in the Great War, he had never been employed anywhere else. His reward for devoted service to the firm was the archetypical gold watch and, with that, he disappeared to spend the rest of his days at his bungalow in Hove, Sussex or some other quiet cliffside estate on England's South Coast.

I was horrified by such a fate. Is that all there is? Will I end up like him?

How can I avoid the same destiny as this office worker straight out of a Dickens novel? It took me a while to figure out the answers. My experiences at the London and Lancashire Insurance Company were repeated several times in my subsequent jobs until I was able to force myself to face the tough decisions as an entrepreneur. I liked working in London and I still thought that people would respect me more because I worked in The City. So, I took the next job that came along, which was with Iwell Engineering, a company manufacturing and exporting abattoir equipment. Their office happened to be next to the Old Bailey—the Central Criminal Court in England and Wales. The Old Bailey is the courthouse named in Charles Dickens' book, A Tale of Two Cities. Above the main entrance of this historic stone building is inscribed the counsel, "Defend the Children of the Poor & Punish the Wrongdoer."

Iwell Engineering was an old fashioned British company, with a factory in the north of England, a sales office in London and customers throughout the world. We supplied stunning pens for Egyptian abattoirs, kosher knives for rabbis in Israel, and rendering boilers for customers stretching from Africa to Australia. The company's international reach seemed exciting until I realised that my role would never extend beyond my office in London.

It would have been obvious that I was not fully absorbed in my new career at Iwell Engineering, because during my extended lunch hours I would sneak off and go next door to sit in the public gallery at the Old Bailey. I relished the legal dramas unfolding on the courtroom floor below. In one such case, a group of bank robbers was conducting its own defence. This was so much more interesting than planning to equip slaughter houses in Russia. Perhaps I should have aimed for a career in law, but I was too young to determine this and my social background and education in the England of that era would have almost certainly ruled this out.

I spent several months struggling to be the future achiever at Iwell Engineering. Then during one lunch hour, I happened to pass the Royal Navy's recruiting office, on Tottenham Court Road. Ideal escape fantasies flooded into my head and, without hesitation, I walked through the door, ready to sign on. Those days of press gangs were long gone, otherwise as a willing new recruit I would have been in for life. Now, however, the Navy required a minimum service time of twelve years from a new recruit. To this 18-year-old, twelve years might as well be for life. Even with images of Pacific islands and exotic ports floating in my mind, I was not going to tie myself up like that.

But I soon discovered that the Royal Air Force would take me on for as little as three years and, not just that, they would train me as an air radar fitter, one of their highest paid tradesmen. I took the job application form home and told my mother that I was joining the RAF. She was aghast, but unable to put up any serious opposition when I pointed out that her own brother, Uncle Dick, had flown with Bomber Command during World War II.

Thus, I left the employ of Iwell Engineering and became one of Her Majesty's Brylcream Boys. For me, another exciting page in life had been turned. Travel was a large part of my motivation for joining the RAF and the training would turn out to be the real benefit of my time in the air force. The military training stuck so well that, even today, I still can jump to attention and shout my service number: "4260980, Sir!" But it was the trade training that would set me up for a future in the computer industry.

During my service in the RAF, I took up the trombone again, an instrument I had played at school. My teacher in school was an ex-bandmaster from the Royal Military School of Music and he tried hard to persuade me to apply for a scholarship there. I didn't feel confident enough at the time to attempt such a thing, which was typical of my thinking about a lot of things at school. But when I arrived for basic training at RAF Bridgenorth, I joined the station band and played with a number of professional musicians who were conscripts rather than regular airmen. That's when I discovered the side benefit that bandsmen were excused from route marches in order to attend band practice. After basic training, I moved into trade training at RAF Yatesbury and again I joined the band as soon as I arrived. At Yatesbury, I also signed up with a traditional jazz band and started playing regular gigs at pubs and other service clubs in the area. My final posting was

RAF Sealand where I played in both the military band and a jazz band.

My desire for foreign travel was so strong that I volunteered for the most unpopular overseas postings available in the RAF—places like the island of Gan, in Addu Atoll in the middle of the Indian Ocean, or Aden, in what is today Yemen. Alas, I was posted to Wales, which taught me how little control I have over my life within a large organisation. But whoever it was, in the RAF administration, making the decision that I should be sent to North Wales had no idea how this would influence my life.

In Wales, I met May, who became my wife and mother of my children. May and her twin sister, Grace, were the daughters of Bill and Elsie Jones. Bill had spent his life working in the steelworks of John Summers and Sons, on the River Dee, just south of Liverpool. Bill and Elsie's traditional lifestyle differed markedly from the one that had shaped me, growing up around London. Elsie lived to serve her husband in every way available to her. I recall her telling me that, in the early years of their marriage, she and other wives would take jugs of beer into the steelworks, for the husbands to slake their thirst at lunchtime.

May's upbringing was patterned along those lines. She learned how to treat her man, most probably having adopted the dictum, "The way to a man's heart is through his stomach." I was quite unprepared for this treatment, having grown up with a working mother and attending a school where girls were considering careers that were traditionally the domain of males. But I succumbed to May's attention and she got her man. Not long after, Alexandra was born and then Richard eased into our expanding young family.

An experience during my time at RAF Sealand red-flagged a career path that I definitely did not want to follow. A group of us was invited to take a tour of the Point of Ayr Colliery which, in 1962, was one of the last remaining deep coal mines in Wales. The coal field extended under the Irish Sea, so that all of the mining took place deep under the sea bed. It would not help the confidence of the miners to know that a nearby coal mine at Mostyn had closed, in 1884, after the mine was inundated with sea water, killing everyone at work that day. Furthermore, Point of Ayr was located less than 30km from the Gresford Colliery which was the site of one of Britain's worst disasters, in 1934, when 266 miners died after an explosion and fire.

Point of Ayr Colliery was also one of the last coal mines to be mechanised and when we went down the mine, they still used pit ponies. Reading the records of the Gresford disaster, even that mine was more mechanised in 1934 than the Point of Ayr Colliery was in 1962. At Point of Ayr, coal was shovelled by hand into tubs and each pony would haul two of these tubs along the rail lines, loaded with a tonne of coal. I didn't know who to feel more sorry for, the ponies or the miners.

As soon as we entered the cage to take us down the shaft it was obvious that this place hadn't changed in 50 years. The word cage was appropriate because it was just a platform supporting a cage on which men stood for the ride to the coal face some 300 metres below. We became airborne as soon as the cage dropped and the light was so feeble we could hardly make out the rock and timber walls as we descended. When we arrived, below, we visited the safety office to be assured that standards had improved since 1934. This was encouraging. The safety briefing was followed by a tour of the stables. The ponies were Welsh mountain ponies and they would typically spend 20 years, or most of their lives, underground. Later, when the men were given longer summer holidays, the ponies came up to the surface once a year but they found it difficult to handle the bright light after a life underground. I remember being told that the ponies understood commands only in Welsh since this was the language used by most of the miners.

From the bottom of the shaft to the coal face was a long walk along dark, steeply graded, satanic tunnels. The coal face itself was a chaotic scene of fallen coal, haphazard timber supports, electrical wiring, ventilation ducts, railway lines, tubs and a pit pony. In the middle of it all, colliers stripped to their underwear in the heat and toiled with shovels to clear a recent blast site. The strobing of the light from the helmet lamps only added to the eerie spectacle. It was like something from a biblical scene of hell.

Our group of air force cleanskins was stricken speechless by the setting and we were more than willing to retrace our steps back to the pit shaft. I can still feel the emotion of climbing back up a long, steep tunnel, gasping for breath with my head banging on rocky outcrops, just as a miner going off shift strode past us as if on a parkland stroll. I was a fit 20-year-old and this chap was probably twenty years older. It is amazing what the human body can get used to. As for the pit ponies, I have no idea how they managed to navigate through the constricted space of these dark, steep, access tunnels. The tunnels were a labyrinth in which it would be easy to get lost but I was told that the ponies knew their way back to the stables.

After that visit, I have always stomached mixed feelings about coal mining. I have great respect for the tough life miners endure, but I have to ask myself why they do this; the visit made me thankful that I didn't need to take up coal mining as a way of life.

I was not the ideal serviceman. I left the RAF with an unblemished record but I was never cut out for Flight Sergeant, much less Air Vice-Marshall. I enjoyed my three years and feel proud to have served in the RAF but, like a conscript, I counted down the days to demobilisation and when that day arrived I burned my uniform. It must have been a reaction to the regimentation and direction of the large organisation.

CHAPTER 3

CHANGING UNIFORMS

LEAVING THE ROYAL AIR Force in 1963 with my trade qualifications proved to be a great opportunity for finding, what was for me, a good job. Data processing was the new buzz word and although I didn't understand what it meant, someone else in a big, respected organisation did. IBM wanted me. I was hired as a Data Processing Customer Engineer and sent for fourteen weeks' training in their engineering school at Rayners Lane, Middlesex. The company was newly established in the United Kingdom, after the local company, ICT, had ceased to be the exclusive distributor for IBM's products. IBM United Kingdom was modelled on the American way of doing business, creating a refreshing and motivating environment that was absent from the staid British organisations I had worked for. Hiring and advancement within the company was based on merit, and not on your accent or what school you had attended. IBM insisted that its customers treat IBM employees as if they were management within their own organisations. Accordingly, all IBM employees followed a strict dress code of dark-blue suits and white shirts. Once, during my engineering training, I was pulled aside and warned not to wear a pin-striped shirt again. Such was the high team morale within the company that I willingly accepted this directive.

For five years, I was a loyal and enthusiastic employee at IBM United Kingdom. I had achieved success in supporting some of IBM's key accounts and I was involved in many successful takeovers of old ICT installations. I was on the winning team and when we saw the ICT engineers, in their greasy overalls, dismantling their old, punched-card machines for replacement by our modern, blue and grey computers, we couldn't help feeling proud to be IBMers. You might almost understand the sentiments of former IBMers who used to meet each morning to sing IBM songs like "Ever Onward, IBM!"

Later in my life, IBM figured at the opposite end of the business spectrum from the companies that I would go on to build or run. But IBM became a paragon which stayed with me throughout my career as an entrepreneur. It was their human resources practices which had the most influence on me. The way IBM recruited people, the idea of promotion from within, employee reviews, open-door policies, suggestion program, employee benefits and the social interaction within the team, all had a profound effect on how I ran my businesses. For most of my entrepreneurial life, I have adopted the same system used by my former IBM managers to conduct employee reviews.

IBM also gave me the managerial skills to succeed in all my small business ventures, and achieve financial independence. I learned to recruit staff who could accomplish great things, allowing them the freedom to create new ways of helping customers. At times, I lost some very good employees to other opportunities, but it was rewarding to know that I had helped these people get ahead in life.

I had been hired by the Liverpool office of IBM, only because this was the location where I was demobilised by the RAF. I was thankful to get a good job, but it was not my choice to live in that part of Britain. I found out later that I could have asked for a position with IBM in London or elsewhere because my skills and experience were valued highly. But the IBM Liverpool manager had quickly grabbed me as an employee, before I could appreciate that my employment location was negotiable. It was another lesson learned the hard way: always determine your strengths and use them to negotiate the desired outcome for yourself.

This location factor became the catalyst for my desire to move from IBM UK to better things. Just as my wish to travel was the raison d'être for signing up with the Royal Air Force, I now began to seek opportunities which would involve travel. I volunteered for temporary duty in Israel, where IBM Customer Engineers were required in order to replace Israelis who had been conscripted into the army during one of the many Arab-Israeli wars.

I also applied for positions at the IBM labs at Hursley, in Hampshire, and at the Montpellier factory in France. Eventually, I became interested in moving to North America to experience working there. It was too difficult to obtain a United States working visa but Canada would willingly offer me the right to live and work there. At about this time, I met a Canadian IBM employee who confirmed that IBM Canada would offer me a job on the spot if I turned up in Canada. But IBM Canada didn't want to be seen poaching the employees of their colleagues across the Atlantic. I took a calculated risk, resigned from IBM UK and applied for the job in Canada

CHAPTER 4

CONTINENTAL SHIFT

I DISCOVERED THAT A visa to work in Canada would give me the option of choosing where in Canada I might live. IBM Canada indicated that they needed Customer Engineers throughout this huge country. The Canadian immigration authorities were pushing Ottawa as a preferred destination for skilled immigrants and they tried to sell me on all the benefits of living in the nation's capital.

But I had learned a hard lesson from joining IBM Liverpool, after leaving the RAF, and not questioning the work location offered to me by IBM UK. Vancouver was my choice for taking up a new job with IBM Canada. But I did hedge my bets by traveling to British Columbia via Toronto and making an appointment with the National Manager of Customer Engineering in Don Mills, Ontario. I told him I was on my way to Vancouver and that I was interested in job opportunities there. My family and I had an arrangement to stay temporarily with my brother's sister-in-law, who lived in North Vancouver.

That meeting resulted in a position for me in Victoria, British Columbia, looking after the provincial government's computer centre. I was unsure where Victoria was but I agreed to take a trip there and check out this opportunity. I spent the next four enjoyable years in British Columbia's capital; thus, I had negotiated the best position I could achieve for my circumstances. I don't know of any school that teaches strategic negotiation skills and I think these can be learned only by getting them through hard-knocks experience and working things out for oneself. Procrastination would be the worst enemy of such a learned skill.

So, we set up home in what I now consider to be the very best city in Canada. It has a marvellous climate, with mild winters and gorgeous summers, and is located in a beautiful part of the world. I was told that I would love it because it is so English. But I don't think I met a single English migrant during my entire stay there. I did work with many Canadians whose parents or grandparents had emigrated from England or a former British colony, so I imagine that Victoria gained its "Englishness" prior to World War II or from the influx of English war brides of Canadians who had served in Europe. Victorians hung onto that reputation with quaint imitations of an English way of life, like replicas of Anne Hathaway's Cottage, performing Pearly Kings, and a restaurant that required patrons to sing along to old British music-hall airs.

My new job was much like the one I had held in England: same computers; different serial numbers. The biggest change was working and living in a different country, with noticeable cultural variations. The negatives I had observed in the United Kingdom, such as class-consciousness and knowing one's place in society were non-existent in Canada. The American management style and structure, in almost all Canadian organisations, was refreshing and stimulating to me. As a result, I became more self-confident and ambitious. While still a loyal IBMer, my first option was to explore opportunities for growth and advancement within the company. This made me realise how complex an organisation like IBM is and how thoroughly compartmentalised the organisational structure was. Everything seemed to operate on a need-to-know principle. For instance, my enquiries about the roles and responsibilities of people in other departments received puzzled reactions from management: "Why would you need to know that?" Soon, I began to feel that I was outgrowing my designated role at IBM. I was getting anxious to face some tougher challenges.

I began reading widely about how IBM and similar organisations were established and how they came to adopt the structures they had. I read the authorised and unauthorized biographies of IBM's founder, Tom Watson, describing what he had learned from the business at the National Cash Register Company before going on to establish International Business Machines prior to World War II. In both accounts of his life, he was portrayed as a successful businessman to be admired, but the unauthorized version planted the seeds of undoing for this loyal IBMer. I asked myself, how could such a company—a leader in business ethics—have evolved from the cutthroat business activities, described in this second version, during its early days?

Several of my IBM colleagues had outside business interests. Dave Lay spent his lunch hours with a stockbroker and could be relied on to supply the occasional tip on some hot, new mining investment. I reconnected with Dave, some 30 years later, and discovered that his early retirement from IBM had led to several unsuccessful business ventures until he fell back on his skills for picking a rising stock. Reverting to the thing that he did so well resulted in a good outcome for Dave and his wife, Verna. When I met him in later life he was able to guide me to another of my successful business ventures, which shows the importance of maintaining good networks. Another IBM colleague, Gary Ross, and I worked on several unsuccessful attempts to develop a new children's toy which was supposed to take the world by storm and match the success of the Hula Hoop. We built several prototypes and thought we were close to launching a new venture, but our efforts were as close to building a successful business as buying a lottery ticket is to becoming a millionaire. We relished the entrepreneurial dream of starting a business but, without confronting the hard parts and dealing with them, it would remain a dream. What was needed was a firm commitment that would include giving up our security at IBM and taking a huge gamble on our idea. We decided against it and it was probably the right decision, but it was another lesson for me that entrepreneurial dreams require doing the hard things and toughing it out until success is achieved.

Readers might find it hard to identify with some of the feelings I have expressed because what's hard for one person can be relatively easy for another. Let me offer a non-business example. Some people have a natural talent for sport. Typically, we first encounter such people at school, where their talents shine and friends and members of the opposite sex are easily attracted. Sport for them comes naturally, whereas for the less talented, playing sport might mean doing hard things and needing to tough it out before being noticed. I was one of those, when growing up, but this encouraged me to excel in other areas. I concentrated on music, which taught me just as much about teamwork as would, say, playing on the school football team. But retreating to activities where the competition is less intense, is not the answer to making a success of one's life. The key is picking something that you can do and applying yourself to overcome any physical or mental limits to your performance. Sometimes this can be very hard.

IBM encouraged employees to work on improving their skills in all sorts of areas. I chose to take several short courses conducted by the Dale Carnegie organisation. These helped me with public speaking and generally with more effective communication. IBM paid for a completed training program and offered paid leave to attend those seminars. I was constantly taking other internal training courses developed by IBM, most of which required me to be away for weeks at training centres in Toronto or Los Angeles. These were primarily for technical training on new computer systems but I also received marketing training so I could assist in selling the benefits of IBM's service.

Reliability, Availability and Serviceability were the key features in their marketing buzzword RAS.

One management training course had a lasting impact on me and would be beneficial in my future business ventures. Trainees played the roles of managers and employees. Each person had a different script and, in one scenario, the manager was required to direct an employee needing to climb a ladder. The employee's script specified that he had a fear of heights and that he had an even bigger fear of admitting it. The hard thing for the employee to face was climbing that ladder but an even harder thing was disclosing the phobia. The manager either had to encourage the employee to face that fear or he had to find a compromise solution to get around the problem in a different way. For the manager, the difficult thing was that his script did not even mention the employee's phobia.

So, here I am in 1972, building a successful career at IBM, with the possibility of moving up the organisational ladder to achieve an income far above what I might have expected when I had left school. In spite of all this, I am not satisfied. I want to do more—much more—and I believed I could do it. Ironically, the words of IBM's founder, Thomas J. Watson, were starting to guide my thoughts: "If you stand up and be counted, from time to time you may get yourself knocked down. But remember this: A man flattened by an opponent can get up again. A man flattened by conformity stays down for good."

I had a few like-minded friends working at IBM and I quickly discovered who they were. We joined in a number of clandestine meetings to discuss various businesses that could be developed. In those days, IBM's monopoly was being challenged by independent manufacturers of disk drives and tape systems that could operate on IBM mainframes at a much lower cost. Also, leasing companies could offer cheaper solutions for the IBMs rented by corporations. These new market developments were made possible by a consent decree that IBM had signed with the

United States government enabling other firms to have access to information that would allow them to compete with IBM.

Since we were Customer Engineers supporting the IBM mainframe computers widely used by large organisations, our private meetings focused on offering an alternative maintenance company. As if reading our minds, IBM promoted me to an RAS marketing representative and taught me to sell IBM's service in the event that a business, like the one we were secretly planning, became a reality in Canada. One of my colleagues, Dave Howard, was sent on a course to study the first competitor of this kind to appear in the United States—Comma, Inc. (Comma being an acronym for Computer Maintenance). The IBM consent decree ensured that we would have a guaranteed supply of spare parts if our planned business venture ever became a reality. To pun a little, the chips were being moved into place and my colleagues and I would soon be faced with the decision to quit IBM or forever remain within the corporate life.

We began to meet more frequently to discuss the possibilities of starting a Canadian version of Comma. Some of those meetings felt as though we were plotting a revolution. I had three co-conspirators and, except for me, all were based in Vancouver. So, I spent many weekends taking the ferry across from Vancouver Island to Vancouver, with my family, and meeting with Dave Howard, Bill Pike and Bill Beaubien. All of us had at least eight years of experience at IBM and were considered to be valuable employees of the company. We knew that launching a Canadian equivalent of Comma, Inc. would have a major impact on IBM Canada and affect our relationships with the friends we had worked alongside at IBM.

One weekend, while returning to Victoria on the Sunday-evening ferry, I was horrified to see my boss and his wife on the same sailing. He seemed pleased to see me and was glad to have someone to chat to during the 90-minute ferry ride.

"So, what have you been up to, this weekend, John?" asks Ray Cronmiller.

"Oh, just catching up with friends," I reply.

Ray was a great guy; I respected him and I wish now that I could sit down with him and share that yarn about what I had really been doing in Vancouver. That, alas, will never be possible; a few years after that ferry ride Ray died of cancer. At the time, it was extremely difficult to have to lie to the people I liked working with, but if I was to go ahead with the business venture there was no choice.

Within a week of that chance ferry encounter with my boss, I reached the point of a make- or-break decision. I could abandon my plans and return to corporate life or I could take that irreversible step into the unknown. In retrospect, I don't know how I did it. It was one of the hardest decisions I have ever made. I walked over to Ray's office to break the news to him that I was leaving IBM and going out to become a competitor. I suppose that IBM managers are trained for such situations because Ray Cronmiller handled the situation very professionally. A few papers were signed, keys were handed over, and I was accompanied downstairs to the main entrance of the office building. Ray gave me a parting handshake; I went home to contemplate my future.

The door that closed behind me had an overwhelming sense of finality. I drove the twenty minutes home with emotions swinging from one extreme to another. I had done it; I was out on my own! But now I no longer had a regular pay cheque; how long would it be before I and my partners could generate enough income to pay ourselves? And I wasn't alone; I had a wife and three children to think of, as well.

I needed to pull myself together before reaching home, so that May would not detect the doubts that lurked in my mind. To my surprise, May appeared to have complete confidence in me and shared none of my hidden concerns. She had moved with me to

Canada and that had been successful, so perhaps she felt I would be just as successful in this next venture. She was good friends with Dave Howard's wife, Elaine, who also had great faith in her husband, thus May and Elaine probably supported each other's views that the new venture would be a success.

Of greater consequence to May would have been the loss of so many good friends. Working for IBM was more than a job and the decision to leave their employment also meant giving up a network of close friends. From that moment, I had no contact with most of my former workmates, until I caught up with some of them 30 years later. That loss probably affected May much more than the realisation that my partners and I were taking a gamble by setting out on our own.

Having made the decision, the time had come to make the decision right. During my long entrepreneurial life, I did learn a few things. One of them is this: Don't worry about whether you have made the right decision; but make the decision right. We recognise many people for being able to make good decisions, but I wonder whether that's simply because they are decisive, and then become very good at making that decision look like the right one.

CHAPTER 5

✱

BREAKING OUT

THE VERY NEXT DAY, I travelled to Vancouver to meet with my new business "partners" and discuss our ensuing strategies. Among us was not a single businessman, just four extremely capable computer engineers with dreams of building an organisation and getting wealthy. We could picture Comma Services Ltd. as a very successful company but we had no idea about how to make that a reality. None of us had worked in sales, finance, advertising, public relations or general administration. Dave Howard was elected president of our new company, I was chosen as the marketing manager, and the two Bills would bring their technical expertise to the operation of the company.

We were typical of four individuals making their first attempts at building a business. We shared an ability to visualise an extraordinary future for all stakeholders, which today would be called the company vision. But we lacked the ideas for developing strategies to get us there—the company mission.

Originally, we had received encouraging comments from potential customers but when they were approached about signing a maintenance agreement with our new company, we discovered that things were not that simple. Government departments had to go to tender for such decisions and private organisations required management decisions at many different levels. One organisation that made the commitment to do business with us was the British Columbia Institute of Technology (BCIT), in Vancouver.

In spite of the confidence boost we received from BCIT, the cold, hard facts of our situation soon became clear. We added up our meagre personal investments in our company—the sum total of all the personal wealth the four of had accumulated—and realised that we each would be living on a much lower income than we had previously enjoyed, with a correspondingly clipped lifestyle. Bill Beaubien had an accountant friend, Wendel Meyer, who had enough faith in us to buy into our company as a partner, but only as an investor, not as an employee of the company. Now, there were five of us to determine the future of Comma Services.

I would now need to leave Victoria, on Vancouver Island, where I had lived happily for more than four years. With very few prospective customers in Vancouver on the horizon, I decided to relocate to Canada's largest city, Toronto, and start a company branch there. This meant moving without my wife and family. The tough life had begun in earnest.

My planned move to Toronto was a challenge to make the best of a 4,000-kilometre road trip at the lowest cost to the new company. Dave Howard had a Volkswagen Beetle and he and I would drive it across the world's second-biggest country, calling on prospects along the way. When we got to Toronto, we would find a two-bedroom apartment where I could live and my partners in British Columbia could support me when visiting me from time to time. The Beetle would be the corporate car to use in Toronto. We would establish a small office to get us started and call upon every IBM user in Toronto. This relocation decision was the first positive move by our new team and it signalled that we were on our way. Sometimes, just making a decision removes the stress from a situation.

I returned to Victoria to put our house on the market and to prepare for an extended stay away from the family. If I could time the sale of the house with the purchase of a home in Toronto, there would be a minimum of disruption to the family. Since it was now early summer, with a bit of luck my kids would be in school by September. Of my three children, two of them were of school age. Family relationships should always take precedence over business activities if you are to achieve a good life balance, but there is a fine line to tread if you are to achieve success. Every situation is different, so no advice can be given without knowing the chemistry of personalities between a potential entrepreneur and his or her spouse.

Dave Howard and I set off for Toronto. We had sales calls to make in Alberta, Saskatchewan and Manitoba, and this meant changing from jeans and t-shirts into business suits when visiting prospective clients. We would hide the Volkswagen to give the impression that we had flown in for the meeting. The most memorable visit of that trip became one of the biggest milestones for our new company. We had arranged a meeting with the management of the computer centre at the University of Manitoba, in Winnipeg. As usual, we parked our car some distance away from the building where we were awaited, changed into business suits, grabbed our briefcases and headed off for the board room where the meeting was held. Dave and I sat with eight people and I was quite jittery; I remember refusing a cup of coffee because my hand might tremble and my nervousness would show. Dave "volunteered" me to be our company's spokesman; I had been pushed forward and hopefully I could achieve the outcome we were working for.

We discovered that they had a maintenance-related problem where they needed the kind of help we could provide; could we support their disk systems which had been supplied by Control Data Corporation? One has to remember that the contract for the maintenance of one set of disk drives would generate enough revenue to support an onsite engineer, so this prospective client had our interest. The problem was that we had no idea whether we could purchase parts and technical manuals from

Control Data, so we could promise the University nothing more than taking the matter up with Control Data's national office in Toronto. At the time, we did not know that this was to become one of our biggest opportunities after we learned all about cooperative marketing.

We left, feeling we had achieved some progress, but no major step forward. We returned to the car and changed into clothes that were more comfortable for the 2,000-kilometre drive from Winnipeg to Toronto. As we pulled out of the parking lot and passed the building where the meeting took place, the group we had been talking to came through the door of the building and headed toward us. I had never before seen a Volkswagen Beetle spin around in such a tight circle; Dave almost bent the car in half. The myth of the Comma Services executives flying into Winnipeg for the meeting was almost blown. Image can mean everything in business and our exposure as a couple of almost-broke dreamers, driving across Canada, could have destroyed any credibility we had gained in the previous hour. It was a close shave. We headed out to the Trans Canada Highway leading to Toronto, determined to meet with Control Data when we got there.

In Toronto, we set up an office and an apartment in Mississauga, conveniently located near Toronto Airport, which we vowed to use for all future cross-Canada journeys. The weeks that followed were filled with administrative tasks—getting phones, business cards, letterheads, desks, chairs and so forth. The apartment also needed to be furnished so that it could accommodate a couple of bachelors.

Building a business is also an exercise in building character and the lessons that were learned came from the landlord of our new office. He was an elderly Jew of Polish origin by the name of Aaron Shostack. When I was a boy, I recall hearing nothing but good things from my mother about the Polish airmen who flew out of Britain's air bases during the Battle of Britain, helping to defend us against Germany's aerial attacks. I also remember the reports about the 22,000 Polish army officers murdered by the Russians in the Katyn Forest, while the captured Polish soldiers were sent to gulag labour camps in Siberia. Aaron was among these soldiers.

He was a colourful character who had suffered a great deal of hardship and he would tell me about life in the gulag. When his sentence was up, he was forced to make his own way back to Poland, mostly on foot, where he applied for refugee status in Canada. He arrived in Canada in the early 1950s, penniless and knowing no one. His first move was to find a synagogue and get some assistance. The Jewish people have the most effective networking system in the world. By the time we met him, Aaron was one of the largest property owners in that part of Toronto. Aaron got some of his associates to supply our new office needs at a good price. This was the stereotypical Jewish business deal but it was a win-win situation for us. Whenever he and I drove back and forth along Toronto's Highway 401 in his Oldsmobile Delta 88, the air conditioning was turned up so high that a fog would be pouring out of the vents.

Aaron helped us fill our non-working hours and would invite us to his home for a meal, then take us to his synagogue. This was obviously a wealthy place of worship and resembled a well-appointed modern theatre. After donning a borrowed yarmulke I sat with him in armchairs which, if used in a Christian church, would put half the congregation to sleep. Aaron gave us a running commentary of the service, from the opening of the holy ark and the procession of the Torah around the congregation, until the end, when it was returned to it's sacred place. His life and example in overcoming huge obstacles and achieving success, yet still offering a helping hand to a couple of young businessmen, starting out as entrepreneurs, is still an inspiration to me.

Moving to Toronto was proving to be the right decision for Comma Services. The city had Canada's largest concentration of IBM computer installations and we needed every one of those prospects if we were going to survive. Our company would not have got off the ground in Vancouver. Dave Howard also decided to relocate to Toronto, and was followed not long after by Bill Pike. Bill Beaubien would stay in Vancouver to take care of our only customer there, the British Columbia Institute of Technology.

The tasks facing us were almost overwhelming and required learning new skills. We needed to determine what services we would offer, set the prices and service terms of agreements, and what we would charge for time and materials services. Legal agreements had to be developed and since our business was the pioneer in a new field, we could not model our arrangements on those of any other company. Promotional material had to be produced and strategies developed to get us in front of the key decision makers. Often it would come down to straight cold calling and trying to persuade the prospect to hear our sales pitch for a service option that he had never heard of. It was an exercise I hated, but one that had to be done. I received my fill of rejections in those early days and it was a struggle not to take them personally.

At the same time, we had to develop budgets and policies for how money was spent, all the while fearfully monitoring our company's fast-diminishing bank balance, to determine how much longer we could stay in business. None of us had an accounting background and we lacked the knowledge needed to accurately forecast our cash requirements. As so often happens, a good Samaritan came along to give us invaluable advice which led to our next success. I had called upon a venture capital company to see if they would be interested in making an investment in Comma. But the timing was not right with this particular venture capitalist. Most such companies manage only a few investments at a time and this one currently had enough on its plate. The person I had met with was very sympathetic and helpful. He gave me the business plan for a company in which they had invested—one of the earliest home-improvement centres which later expanded across Canada. He asked me to keep the business plan confidential but suggested that, if we wanted to attract a venture capitalist, we should produce a document like that.

I took the business plan to my partners and we pored over several hundred pages of market analysis, profit-and-loss forecasts, cash-flow projections, staffing plans, property and fixed-asset requirements, and what today would be called a SWOT (strengths, weaknesses, opportunities, threats) analysis. It was a daunting task to produce a similar document for our company but, after burning the midnight oil over this new "bible" of ours, a week or two later, we developed a business plan. The results confirmed our worst fears. Having relocated to Toronto in midsummer, our analysis showed that, without a significant investor, we would not survive past Christmas. All efforts would now be channelled into finding an investor.

Just three months had elapsed since I resigned from IBM but so much had taken place that it was hard to comprehend and sort out what was important and what was not. In the meantime, my house in Victoria had been sold and I found a house to rent in Mississauga.

Toronto's higher property values, in comparison to Victoria, constrained my options to what I could afford to rent. I wanted a house that gave the appearance we were doing well, more to convince myself and May of this fact, than to impress others. I settled for the best street in a lower-cost neighbourhood, close to the Zellers discount department store and the local, government-run Liquor Control Board of Ontario outlet. May and the children joined me in October, 1972—along with our Dalmatian dog, Cheetah, who had been with us since leaving England—and prepared for the adventure of experiencing an Ontario winter. After living through Victoria's mild winters, it meant exchanging raincoats for parkas and bicycles for ice skates. The furniture followed them by road. The only upset of the move, for May, came after the furniture had arrived: all of her precious indoor plants had frozen during their Canadian odyssey across The Prairies.

But our business family at Comma Services was not getting along as it should. We often spent more energy in the disagreements among us than we did in building the business. This business partnership was a lesson in human nature, watching how one partner would connive with another and then ambush a meeting with a suggestion for a change in direction. Dave Howard was the president but he had never managed a team before, let alone directed the growth of a company. Bill Pike added very little to the business side of things, outside of the technical area, at which he excelled. Bill Beaubien and Wendel Meyer were still in Vancouver and dropped in on the Toronto office only occasionally. I vowed to myself that if I got through this venture, I would never again go into a partnership. Some partnerships can work, but five partners in a start-up situation is very difficult.

Despite the on-going battles between partners, I look back on this period as one of the most satisfying of my life. Until then, I had always been a small cog in a very big wheel and the big wheels were a major insurance firm, the Royal Air Force and IBM. Now, I was a huge cog in a very small wheel. I had to perform tasks I had never done before, some of which were absolutely critical to the company's survival. It was a challenge I rose to and one which gave me great satisfaction. It showed me what people can do if given the opportunity—and the freedom to tough out the hardships that come with it.

CHAPTER 6

OPEN TO CHANGE

THIS PHASE OF MY life taught me the need to be ready at all times to review and modify an existing business plan. Comma Services had been started by four computer technicians, all with approximately the same background and experience. We each had some input to the company's business plan but, having the same background, the business would mirror the jobs we had performed at IBM. We needed to pick up other opportunities and create a business that was tailored more to the market. We had to listen to what the customers really wanted and modify our offering accordingly.

At that time, a market for second-hand computers was developing. Keep in mind that we were operating in the mainframe era, when a single computer, like the IBM 370/155, would cost in excess of two million dollars. Companies like Greyhound Leasing would buy used computers and lease them to new customers in revised system configurations. This new market development created the need for a company that could offer refurbishment services and install or remove features to suit the needs of the new customer. A service such as this required a factory where systems could be dismantled, reconfigured, and repainted to look new. None of this was in our original business plan and it became an essential rethinking of strategy if we wished to succeed.

This reconfiguration work was not always done at the factory. Some systems were so large that it was easier to send an engineer to work on the system than to ship it to the factory. I recall the case of one company that was buying cheque-sorting machines from British banks and selling them to American banks. The machines had to be converted from 240V, 50Hz electric current to 110V, 60Hz current. The firm was located in Minneapolis and I flew down there for a week, in the middle of winter, to carry out the work. There was no book published on how to do this, so our company had to figure it out in advance and order all the correct components. The lesson here is that an entrepreneur needs to react quickly and modify the originally envisioned business plan according to opportunities that arise. But one has to avoid impetuous decisions which will have the company flip-flopping all over the place. It's a fine line between the two but it is something which all entrepreneurs will face, especially in the early days of a new business.

The venture capital market in Toronto, in the 1970s, was small and it didn't take us long to make contact with the key players. It took even less time to determine whether a venture capitalist was tied down with other investments, or that our type of business did not fit into the investor's portfolio. But when I called Charterhouse Canada Ltd. and spoke with George Fells, it was immediately obvious that we had found an opportunity. The timing sounded right and Charterhouse were interested in our industry. Dave and I met with George Fells and one of his investment officers, Gordon Leonard. Charterhouse Canada was a subsidiary of a long-established English financial firm. All four of us at the meeting were English migrants to Canada which generated an instant rapport.

Dave and I left the meeting on a high, having given them a copy of our business plan. Gordon Leonard was assigned as the investigative officer to review our operations at Comma Services and to determine our business potential. If we met their expectations and criteria, a sum of money would be loaned to the company in the form of a debenture with a floating charge over our assets. In other words, it would be secured against everything we owned, now or in the future, even though that would not be enough to repay them in the event of our failure. The loan would be advanced, in stages, against our achievement of certain milestones and interest would be paid at a rate just above the standard bank rates. In return for the added loan risk, Charterhouse would have the option of purchasing 25% of our company's stock at a nominal value, that option to be exercised at a time of their choosing.

We now had about eight weeks of survival left, given our company's current capital, and surely we should be able to get Charterhouse to put in the money by then.

But that was a naive view of how things happen in the corporate financial world. We began a period of endless meetings to enable Gordon Leonard to prepare a report for the Charterhouse Board of Directors, which met in England once a month. Our investment report was slated for the final board meeting of the year. The date of that meeting loomed like the awaited sentence for a man found guilty of first-degree murder. Gordon wanted to meet our Vancouver partners and see the office there, but he had other activities to perform for Charterhouse while in Vancouver. I flew there with him and it was hard not to keep pushing him to share the same sense of urgency we had about our company's situation. We went to the Pacific Stadium, not to see a B.C. Lions football game, but to inspect a new scoreboard which had been installed by a company also being considered by Charterhouse as a venture-capital investment. I couldn't help thinking that this company might be competing for the same funds we were vying for.

Now that Comma Services had a potential investor, we needed to impress Charterhouse with new maintenance contracts being signed regularly, but an Ontario equivalent of our British Columbia Institute of Technology client was proving to be elusive. Then, we discovered a whole group of large and established companies who could benefit from our existence, buying services from us in preference to IBM with whom they were in head-on competition. We were learning the benefits of cooperative marketing.

Our company promptly took advantage of the laws governing the IBM consent decree which allowed us to offer an alternative maintenance service to purchasers of IBM mainframes. At our Mississauga warehouse, we began refurbishing used IBM systems for Greyhound Leasing, upgrading them to include different features and installing the systems for Greyhound's new customers. Nine times out of ten, we would provide the end user with the on-going maintenance service required.

Our marketing efforts had a new focus and, before long, all the major suppliers of add-on peripherals in the IBM marketplace were approaching us about our installation and maintenance services. We used our ever-shrinking funds to fly Bill Pike to various manufacturers in the United States in order to work out the technical aspects of their needs and undergo training when needed. We began working with companies like Cambridge Memories and EMM, makers of large-scale memory systems. This led us to some of IBM's largest Canadian customers—Shell Oil, Sun Life of Canada, and Ryerson Polytechnic (now Ryerson University). Most of these sites had one or two resident IBM engineers, so we now had to work with our former colleagues, but this also gave us the opportunity to size up future recruits for our own company. I am quite certain that my partners and I were the subject of many discussions back at IBM headquarters.

Control Data Canada was another manufacturer selling add-on disk drives to users of IBMs. They ran a leasing company which acquired IBM mainframes, fitted them with Control Data peripherals, and leased these to clients. For this, they needed our firm's refurbishing and mainframe maintenance services. Our customer base was growing but my relationship with Control Data was destined to be much more than that of a customer.

In November, 1972, new business was coming in fast, but despite the increasing revenues, our expenses were mounting even faster and we were facing the prospect of no pay cheque in December—unless Charterhouse came through with some funds. As to my personal finances, I was existing from week to week and I knew that I could not pay the next month's rent. There certainly would be no money to buy Christmas presents for my kids.

What do venture capitalists look for? The private equity capitalist has very different business criteria than those of banks. Banks will lend only against solid assets like property, until they have sufficient confidence in a client. But the venture capitalist is looking at the potential exit strategy while evaluating the initial investment. The exit strategy might be to sell the company down the track, or to take it public. The goal is to invest for the purpose of encouraging the company's growth and then to quickly find a buyer for the invested share in the company. This way, the venture capitalist can take the money and repeat the strategy with another company. From Charterhouse's viewpoint, Comma Services could potentially be sold to one of the many large companies with whom we were now doing business. Therefore, my advice to would-be founders of any start-up company is this: always consider your exit strategy, right from the beginning.

The Charterhouse board of directors, in London, met at the start of December. We were told by telephone that their investment in Comma Services had been approved. All that remained was to wait for the lawyers to draw up loan agreements, personal guarantees, and prepare various other legal documents for filing with a dozen or so government departments. I was praying that these would be completed during December and we would have the first loan instalment before Christmas.

By the middle of December, this looked increasingly unlikely and I was preparing to tell my family there would be no turkey for Christmas. In all my life, I had never been so broke. I grabbed at a straw and, armed with a letter of intent from Charterhouse Canada, went to see the bank manager at the Toronto Dominion Bank. Would he make an unsecured loan to a fellow without a job or pay cheque, and with no assets to offer as security? The TD Bank agreed to prop me up until my next pay was received, and I shall forever be grateful to that bank manager for salvaging Christmas 1972 for us.

The investment by Charterhouse required us to appoint Gordon Leonard to our board and to get their approval for decisions about a long list of matters. This seemed onerous at first, but it turned out to be a blessing in disguise. Given that my partners and I spent more time sorting out our disagreements than building the business, most such arguments were now decided by the umpire, Gordon Leonard. The Charterhouse arrangement imposed the discipline on our company that was lacking until then.

With this sound financial backing for our company, things were made a lot easier all round. We no longer had to skate on thin ice when trying to impress a prospective customer that we were a well-funded business. Comma Services was now backed by a British banking group that had been around as long as Canada had existed. Also, I could now focus a bit more on the non-business aspects of my life. I have always believed in keeping a balance between business, family and friends. Having survived six months during which business was the engrossing, jealous mistress, I wanted to devote time to other dimensions of my being. My family was the most important part of that and all of my non-working hours were spent exploring Toronto with my children. The city offered us far more than Victoria ever did; there were plenty of museums, circuses, skating rinks, pioneer villages, parades and lots of diversions to excite children and adults alike.

CHAPTER 7

✸

BALANCING ACT

ONE THING I DID lack in Toronto; and that was friends. I lost all my Canadian friends when I left IBM and didn't give myself time to develop new friendships in Toronto. My relationships with the partners at Comma were fairly cool. I was aware of a Canadian service club whose membership was restricted to young men aged between 21 and 40. It was The Kinsmen Club and I wrote them for information about the organisation. Soon, I got a call from George Carruthers of The Kinsmen Club of Mississauga inviting me to join him at the next meeting, on a Thursday night. George picked me up in his Cadillac and we went to a local restaurant where the meeting was held. It was an enjoyable evening, punctuated by an amusing form of parliamentary procedure where a Sergeant at Arms imposed fines when someone breached the rules. The club's goal was to serve the community's greatest needs and, in the process, furnish opportunities for fellowship and personal growth. Their philosophy and aims were right up my alley and I joined the club.

Club members represented a wide cross section of the community, including both tradesmen and professionals, and I found the club to be a great outlet for personal growth. I made friends that I will cherish for life. Moreover, it was an ideal networking community and a source of the most creative ideas in our quest to raise money for community projects. One of our members created the first lottery in Canada and later became a consultant to the Canadian government when the 1976 Olympic lottery was started. His name was Ernie Priess and he and I would team up to run a lottery-based business many years later, after I had moved to Australia. Life is one, long networking event and those networks need constant maintenance. So, keep in touch with your old colleagues.

Some Kinsmen Club of Mississauga members were already very successful people, including lawyers and accountants, but there were members who had started at the bottom and, for them, the only way was up. For such members, the Kinsmen organisation fuelled an impressive transformation. Take Randy Scarr, for instance. Randy was a native Canadian who grew up on an Indian reservation. His job was maintaining trucks, although I don't believe he was a qualified mechanic; he was more like an assistant. When he first joined Kinsmen, he had great difficulty expressing himself at meetings; he would stumble over his words and receive a lot of good natured kidding about this from members. Most people in such a situation would probably give up and quit. Not Randy. He threw himself into every project and volunteered his services to anyone who needed a hand. His ability to address club meetings improved dramatically and, gradually, members began to listen and to accept what he was saying. He gained respect for having overcome his earlier difficulties and, within five years, he was elected president of the club. From there, he rose to the next level in the Kinsmen regional hierarchy. Randy Scarr was an outstanding example of what can be achieved by applying oneself fully to any given task and learning the skills that are required. Sadly, in 1979, at the age of 39, he died of a heart attack; he will evermore remain Kin Randy.

Comma Services continued to grow and we opened offices in Montreal and Ottawa. Recruiting staff became the next challenge and, although we did manage to seduce a few more IBM engineers, we would have to expand our hiring program and train our own people. Qualified electronics technicians were not easy to find at that time, so we tapped an overseas source of recruits. We ran a few ads in the United Kingdom, Dave would fly there for the interviews, and pretty soon we had a steady stream of recruits arriving at Toronto Airport and going straight into Bill Pike's training program. The company was blossoming and, although the cost of financing that growth foiled any chance of being profitable, Charterhouse would have been pleased with their new investment. But I don't think Gordon Leonard was pleased with his new role of keeping warring partners on track. We continued to receive the promised injections of funds, even though we did not precisely meet the milestones set down in our original plan.

Our company's relationships with the hardware manufacturers and leasing companies strengthened, over time, because we offered these companies significant marketing advantages they would otherwise not have. Control Data Canada appreciated this advantage more than others and it wasn't long before Tom Forrestall approached us to gauge our interest in selling our company. We had been operating for less than two years and, at the rate we were growing, such an acquisition would be a smart move on his part. As with any venture capital company, from the moment it had invested in Comma Services, Charterhouse was continually assessing opportunities to divest itself of this venture.

We indicated an interest in selling our firm and the Control Data head office in Minneapolis gave Tom Forrestall the authority to make an offer. We were not aware at the time that Control Data had purchased our namesake, Comma Corporation, in the United States. Had we known this, we would have had greater bargaining power for our own company. I think we were willing to sell ourselves short, largely because we were tired of the tension among the company's partners.

The deal closed a lot faster and with a lot less heartache than the original setting up of the company and the financing by Charterhouse. Control Data got their new division, Charterhouse made their profit, and we gained new management positions with Control Data, with an increase in salary to boot. What disappointment I did feel was tempered by the fact that I no longer had to struggle with partnership bickering.

During the two years we were in business, the housing market had gone through the roof. The house I had sold in Victoria for $30,000 was now worth $60,000 and I was now living in a city where housing cost a lot more. My gain from selling my shares in Comma allowed me to buy a house for $80,000 which knocked me back to roughly where I stood financially two years earlier. My real gain was the learning I underwent during those two years. The knowledge and skills gained in building a company, from scratch to a national operation, could not be acquired at a university. These gave me greater confidence that I could do it again in future, but this time, by myself.

Soon, I spotted another opportunity—one which I could undertake on my own. As marketing manager at Control Data, I was receiving regular requests for maintenance services from manufacturers and users of minicomputer systems. The mainframe computers of the past ten years were now facing competition from comparatively small but powerful systems made by Digital Equipment Corporation (DEC) and Data General. These companies produced only the central processing units and they relied on other manufacturers to provide disk and tape storage, printers, and data entry devices. Initially, such systems were adopted by universities and research organisations that were capable of integrating the various components and sorting out the inevitable problems when something went wrong. In addition, DEC and Data General supplied very basic operating system software and programming languages which appealed only to the technical users of computers. There was a big market for such systems in business applications, provided someone could integrate the various components and supply the support and services demanded in a business environment.

I took a proposal to Control Data that our division should become the integrator that I foresaw the market demanded. The response was negative for the Comma Division but, as things turned out, positive for me. I did not have the funds to keep a new company going while I searched for my first customers. I needed to find a customer or a cooperative marketing partner who would serve as a launching pad for such a new business.

Then, I received a phone call from Bob Russell, in Montreal, and I found my launching pad. Bob's company, Minitech Information Systems, was a group of four programmer/analysts which had been developing business systems based on the mixed- vendor minicomputers I described. Their software used an operating system called Micos, developed for Data General computers by a company in Elmsford, New York. They wanted to supply the hardware and software, as a package, but they did not have any hardware expertise. Would I be interested in joining them?

I flew to Montreal, next day, to meet with Bob and his partners. They did not make good first impressions. I am searching for kind words to use, but basically Bob Russell was cross-eyed, Richard Lapointe had one leg, Jock Mullen was a large, bald hippie and Graham McIntyre was a flamboyant man about town. A more unlikely group of guys posing as businessmen I have never seen. Bob put his proposal to me which nearly had me running for the door.

"We want you to come into partnership with us," he said.

They obviously had achieved quite a bit so far, they certainly had the technical ability to create systems, and Graham McIntyre certainly sounded as though he could sell systems. They were my potential launching pad but I could never contemplate a partnership with the Minitech boys.

I carefully explained my experiences, since leaving IBM, and how paranoid I had become about future partnerships, while taking care to assure them that I could see that a partnership with Minitech would be different. I wasn't being honest in that assurance but I did not want to offend them and I did want a business relationship with these guys if at all possible. I outlined a plan where I would form a company which supplied hardware, only, and would never compete with them for software business. The company would sell hardware systems to Minitech at favourable prices, i.e. no other company would get better prices and this would allow Minitech to achieve its goal of supplying complete systems of hardware and software. I stressed the advantages to them of being freed up from the responsibility for hardware, allowing them to focus on what they did best—developing advanced business applications. As I talked, I recall being totally absorbed with the vision I had for my new company and how it's existence would be such a great thing for Minitech.

Eventually I stopped talking and asked them, "What do you think?"

They looked at each other and basically said, "Okay; sounds good."

We were in business. Minitech was very much like that: make a decision and let's get on with it.

CHAPTER 8

ON MY OWN

I RETURNED TO TORONTO, gave my resignation notice to Control Data and began work on launching Integrant Services Limited. Unlike IBM, Control Data did not escort me to the door of the office building. I worked out my notice with them, in order to achieve the best possible handover that I could. Later, it turned out, I would need them.

Starting Integrant was a whole lot easier than starting Comma Services. For one thing, I had a customer who needed me to supply systems almost immediately, so the emphasis was to fulfil those demands rather than chasing after new business. Relationships with suppliers became the priority rather than interactions with customers. At Comma, we were supplying our own labour, with parts and maintenance items being the only purchases. At Integrant, I was selling expensive capital equipment which I had to source and pay for, so I required significant capital or borrowings to do this. I didn't have much personal wealth and the little I had was tied up in my house. But I used my track record as a successful entrepreneur at Comma Services to get my bank manager to approve the maximum loan possible. My wife and I put up personal guarantees and we used our house as collateral. In addition, we were able to obtain loans of up to 50 per cent of inventory and 70 per cent of receivables. Much later, when I worked for 25 years as an entrepreneur in Australia, I was never able to find an Australian banker who could offer me such generous assistance in building my later businesses.

I found myself selling our capabilities to our vendors rather than to customers. Companies like Data General, Centronics Printers, Hazeltine Terminals, and Control Data supplying disk drives became my key partners. My sales pitches to them were every bit as important as selling to a new customer. As a result, they agreed to supply me on credit terms and actively solicited new business for me. This was the kind of partnership I needed, not the shareholder type of partners.

Almost all companies are individual links within a supply chain and only the very biggest corporations control all parts of the chain, from raw materials to end user. Most companies are as dependent on having effective suppliers as they are on obtaining new customers, yet the focus is so often placed on the sales side of an enterprise. Take any advice given on growing a business, and the emphasis is usually on marketing, determining what the customer wants, and developing strategies to attract and keep those customers. The supply side of the business equation is almost always glossed over. During the early development of Integrant Services, my commitment was to one customer, Minitech. Thus, good supplier relationships became the overriding consideration. Accessing the needed products at the right price, getting favourable credit terms, gaining extra support services, featuring in a supplier's promotional activities, and encouraging suppliers to generate business leads are all activities that can be stimulated. This supply-side focus boosted Integrant's success.

At the same time, I had to keep the Minitech boys happy, while keeping a careful watch on what kind of business they were conducting. I didn't have the expertise to fully evaluate the software they proposed to deliver in each particular contract, but I could get a feel for whether they were confident in meeting their obligations. I had to demand prompt payment for the hardware I was supplying, but remain flexible on payment terms when the end user was not paying Minitech. Since Minitech was my only customer, I was walking a tightrope; if they collapsed, I would fall. Broadening my customer base was the obvious answer, but simply keeping up with Minitech's rocketing success was taking all my energies and stretching Integrant to the limit.

I found that I could assist Minitech in the sales process, making myself available as a resource in sales presentations. Four years after making that sales presentation at the University of Manitoba, I was a lot more confident in my ability to persuade.

One of my good decisions was to hire a technical helper who could assemble, install and service the various hardware components of our customized systems. George Coupar had moved to Canada from Scotland and, like Captain Kirk in Star Trek, I now had a Scottish engineer to beam me up. George was a young, very talented electronics technician and, before long, he was designing his own hardware modifications to improve the systems and reduce our costs. We would stage the systems at our Mississauga warehouse, load them in the station wagon, and drive to the customer's location—usually, in Montreal.

It was 1976, preparations for the Montreal Olympics were in full swing, and companies had money to spend on new computers. Minitech had lots of contacts around the city so there was no shortage of challenging system installations. George and I drove between Toronto and Montreal countless times and we worked long hours to complete the installations. I was driven by the instinct of nurturing my own company and George was motivated by the responsibility and authority I had given him. Since then, I have always tried to give employees as much free rein as possible and, nine times out of ten, it pays off.

One of our installations in Montreal was for the Auberge d'Richelieu, a hotel built specifically for the Montreal Olympics. The system we supplied would be one of the first front-office and food-and-beverage systems installed in Canada, and perhaps the world. Until then, most systems had a back-office accounting capability and the front desk relied on stand-alone folio machines looking much like oversized cash registers. We networked the remote terminals located in the restaurants, and at the front desk, to the computer system housed in its own climate-controlled room. This was quite unique since none of today's sophisticated network architecture existed. Each terminal was connected by a twisted pair of copper wires running back to the computer's multi-port interface, designed by George. In addition, the Minitech team had developed quite revolutionary software to handle all the main functions required by the hotel.

With the 1976 Olympic Games about to begin, I was installing and testing the system while tradesmen all around us were hammering, drilling, painting and laying carpets. It was a frantic scene to get everything working properly. When we delivered the system, the hotel's French-Canadian owner swished into the lobby, in his fur coat, and cast a glance at our pride and joy. The manager asked him how he liked the new system and, although I don't understand much French, I could hear the owner say that he didn't like the colour.

The Auberge d'Richelieu became a good referral site for us and it generated interest from other hotel chains. We received orders from various Hilton hotels in Canada, a Hilton property in San Juan, Puerto Rico, and eventually installed a system for Hilton International's flagship hotel, the Waldorf Astoria, in New York.

The next big order came as a result of working with CN Hotels. They wanted a restaurant system in the CN Tower, the world's tallest unsupported structure, being built in Toronto. This was a revolutionary system and the terminals were designed to be waiter stations installed in the revolving part of the restaurant at the 351-metre level of the 555-metre-tall tower. We chose a small terminal from TRW which had a numeric keypad, a printer and a display panel—rather like a large version of todays point-of-sale terminals. This would be used by the waiters to enter orders and print out bills for customers. Each of these terminals had a modem for communicating with the base of the tower, where the computer was installed.

As I was planning the installation, I went up to the restaurant level when it was just a concrete slab suspended from the central core of the tower. It was winter; at 351 metres up, it was freezing and a gale was blowing. I stood, in hardhat, parka and boots, about twenty metres from the edge of that slab and my feet would not budge even an inch closer. Thankfully, what I had come to inspect was located close to the central core of the tower. Our system was as successful as the tower itself and we made the most of the publicity gained from supplying it.

I became good friends with Karl Baker, manager of the CN Tower restaurant, and I persuaded him to join the Kinsmen Club of Mississauga, which had become both an escape from my business and a complementary activity to it. We would put as much effort into getting a fund raising project off the ground as we would devote to the implementation of a new system project. I can still hear Karl's booming voice, shouting out as he sold hamburgers at a Kinsmen Mississauga festival: "Hamburgers! They're lovely!" Almost certainly, the crowd had no idea they were being served by one of Canada's senior hotel executives.

Joining the Kinsmen organisation was a great education for young men. Holders of office and project leaders were all young people trying things for the first time. Kinsmen is affiliated with Apex in Australia and Round Table in England, Africa and India. It was a good recruiting ground for new staff. I hired my first sales manager, Jim Tomkins, a former sales executive at the Polaroid Corporation. "Jimmy T" joined me at Integrant and remained a key employee until, with my approval and support, he left to work for our American supplier and become vice-president of sales, in New York. I never regretted the loss of an employee if he or she had outgrown the position that I could offer and progressed to greater things. It was satisfying to know that I had helped this person move upward in his or her career.

One of the biggest Kinsmen service projects in which I had a hand was organising the 1976 District 8 Convention, held in the Bahamas. We were reaching beyond the norm because such conventions were usually held within the District—at that time Central Ontario and parts of Quebec. We were aiming for something entirely different that would go down in Kinsmen history as one of the best conventions, ever. Normally, a Kinsmen Club would book a resort location and it would be up to members to make their way to the venue and home again. In our case we had to provide the whole package. We chartered three Air Canada jets to take us from Toronto to Freeport with one of the jets originating in Sault Saint Marie, Ontario. We booked the entire Grand Bahama Resort, taking advantage of a slump in their bookings. The convention was a resounding success with every seat taken on all three planes. The Bahamian Minister for Tourism was our guest of honour and our invitation included the Bahamian Police Band. I was president of the Mississauga Kinsmen that year and the convention we had mounted helped me win the Outstanding President's Award.

A tradition of Kinsmen conventions is that the club bidding for the following year's convention hosts a hospitality suite. The bidder was the Sault Saint Marie Club and they wanted to offer their local beer. The Bahamian government would not allow the club to import beer for this purpose but they would allow each air passenger to bring in a carton of 24 bottles. So, the aircraft which flew in from northern Ontario had some 200 passengers bringing with them 200 cartons of Northern Ale beer as carry-on baggage.

Organising that convention taught me a lot about taking on big, imaginative projects but I was amazed at the opposition that our efforts generated. It was, I think, an example of the tall poppy syndrome—the tendency of some to hammer down the nail that stands out. Perhaps our Kinsmen opponents were revealing their envy, since there was a strong campaign against the way we had conceived and put together the convention. The gist of the negative sentiments was that it was unfair to the battlers—the Kinsmen who could not afford to do what the "rich yuppies" of Mississauga could do. That was hardly true and afterwards we received a number of letters from lower-income Kinsmen thanking us for making it possible for them to enjoy their first-ever overseas trip.

I have found similar examples in business, when I have taken on projects which enjoyed some measure of success with the public. There was never a shortage of people trying to knock you down if you were perceived as having achieved prominence. This syndrome of being challenged by parties outside the relationship between buyer and seller is indicative of another problem that business people will often face. Many times during my entrepreneurial career, I have encountered people and special-interest groups, completely unrelated to the actual business function, who want to impose regulation and control over what that business is trying to achieve. This seems to have become more common as society has moved toward greater socialism and the belief that governments should decide what is best for all of us. This is definitely a business dimension that prospective entrepreneurs should prepare for and train themselves to handle.

CHAPTER 9

✶

NETWORKING

IT IS ASTONISHING HOW people will come into and out of one's life, often reappearing much later to present a business opportunity. Nowadays, with the ability to Google a person on the Internet, this is not so surprising. But, for most of my career, nothing like the Internet or search engines existed. You will notice throughout my story that these reappearing individuals have had quite an influence on my life. That's why I'm fond of saying, life is like one, long networking event. In the mid-1970s, Integrant had some spare warehouse space and I could sublet this to John Knorr, a German-Canadian computer terminal salesman. He would reappear much later in my life, after I had migrated to Australia, becoming the European distributor for the company in which I was general manager, and later buying the company from its Australian owners.

It was impossible to foresee such a scenario, then, but meeting John Knorr was definitely an important event. Another salesman calling on Integrant was Stan Tyminski. He reappeared twenty years later like a ghost from my past. One night, during the 1990s, I was watching the evening news on TV in Australia and discovered that a Canadian was running for President of Poland. I could not believe my eyes: it was Stan Tyminski. Alas, he didn't get elected, otherwise I might have been doing business in Warsaw.

Integrant was making exceptional progress during it's first two years of operation. The relationship between Minitech and Integrant was symbiotic thus we complemented each other well. But I knew it was essential to broaden our customer base to ensure that we were not totally dependent on one source of business. Adding to my concerns was the mounting total of outstanding receivables from Minitech. The amount owing was in the order of several hundred thousand dollars and, in 1976, this was a huge sum which, if not recovered, would wipe out Integrant. Canadian banks were far more liberal with their lending policies than is the case with Australian banks; we had a large percentage of our receivables and inventory financed by the bank. Integrant was required to provide the bank manager with monthly reports on outstanding receivables and, as soon as Minitech missed a 30-day payment, alarm bells rang.

We began to spread our risk and signed up a number of new companies, both large and small. It became a significant business in supplying disk systems to upgrade computers from Digital Equipment Corporation, after buying the disks from our old friends at Control Data. Furthermore, our service revenues grew because, with every system sold, there was a new maintenance agreement.

But Minitech continued to worry me. The company didn't bother much with titles but Bob Russell acted, more or less, as the CEO and I kept in close touch with him. He was very open about their financial situation and it became clear they were running on borrowed time. It was not a matter of, if they went bankrupt, but when. I was the major creditor so at any time I could have placed them into liquidation, but that would be cutting off my nose to spite my face. Bob was extremely cooperative about getting his account paid down with us, as much as possible, before the axe fell on Minitech. I imagine he still had hopes of turning things around and, like Mr. Micawber in David Copperfield, he supposed that something would always turn up. Come to think of it, Bob Russell stands out, like the Micawber of Charles Dickens, as an example of survival; I still feel like Micawber's long-suffering wife in that I did not want to desert him. Bob remains a friend to this day.

Bob had a great sense of humour and he used it in the most unlikely ways. I mentioned that his business partner, Richard, had only one leg, having lost the other in a motorcycle accident. When another one-legged computer programmer applied for a job at Minitech, Bob couldn't help himself; he had to hire this guy. It added to the Minitech image and it gave Bob the opportunity to buy one pair of shoes for the two of them.

Once, when visiting New York on business, he took his son along and they did some shopping, taking advantage of the lower prices compared to those in Montreal. While there, he was caught in a torrential downpour and his clothes got soaked. So, he dropped by a men's' wear shop and purchased a new suit and shirt, and stuffed the soaked clothes into a carrying bag. He drove back to Montreal, stopping at the border to clear Canadian Customs. The customs officer found receipts for the items Bob was wearing and had not declared, and for which he would have to pay duties, plus a fine for trying to evade customs duty. Bob considers the amount, decides that the duty is too high and, to the surprise of the customs officer, undresses in the customs hall and forfeits the new suit and shirt to Customs. With a line up of travellers waiting and watching behind him, he unpacks the crumpled and damp clothes from his carry bag and gets dressed.

Minitech's financial problems did not surprise me; what did, though, was how uninformed Minitech's bankers were. They ended up losing a lot more than we did. Had they acted earlier, the situation could have been reversed. This was in sharp contrast to our own bankers who had already ceased lending against the receivables from Minitech.

The slow demise of Minitech was spread over a period of twelve months, and when they went into receivership, we counted our losses but heaved a sigh of relief. Our losses had shrunk our net worth to almost zero. We had survived, we were still solvent, and by then we had plenty of other business to fall back on. We could now run Integrant without the constant worry that our biggest customer would sink and take us under too. The market needed our systems and the services that Minitech had been providing. So, former Minitech employees went into business to take Minitech's place. Wiser for the experience, we established strict credit policies and personal guarantees with these new start-up companies.

Had we been able to stand still and regroup, Integrant Services would have been a very healthy company, but the computer industry does not stand still and we had to reposition to where the growth was, or die. However, we were undercapitalised for the opportunities available to us. We needed to invest in more inventory, train new staff, and expand into new premises. I had borrowed as much money as I could, so it was essential to hunt down other sources of funds.

The systems we were supplying were built around an operating system called Micos, developed by a New York company, Mini-Computer Systems, Inc. (MCS). MCS was a public company whose shares were traded on the predecessor to NASDAQ in New York. MCS had a manufacturing plant in California. Knowing our problems after the demise of Minitech, the president of MCS, Bill Doniger, called me and proposed that MCS should purchase Integrant and make it the Canadian operation for this fast-growing company. Given the pressures of the previous twelve months, the offer sounded attractive. It was a reprieve from the need to tough out the hard things. Alarm bells should have rung but the deal sounded like a win-win opportunity, so I flew to New York to hear what they had to offer. The proposal was to buy my company with MCS shares which, at their prevailing market value, was a very attractive offer. In addition, the company was projecting significant growth and I could see only one direction for the value of the shares—upward.

The only problem was that my shares were in escrow and could not be traded for two years. But I didn't intend to sell my shares for several years. My staff, George Coupar and Jim Tomkins included, were keen to see the sale go ahead and they sensed greater career opportunities in Canada and in the USA as a result of the sale of Integrant. In fact, within two years, Jim would be Vice President of Sales in New York, and George would join the MCS development team.

The sale of Integrant to MCS was an education in the corporate regulation and reporting that go with a publicly owned company. I wish I had taken a photograph of the board room at the lawyer's offices in Toronto when we signed the deal. A table which could accommodate, perhaps, twenty people was covered with piles of documents, stacked six inches high, and all of these papers required my signature. Legal fees and time-consuming reports would become an on-going reality of my new job, running the subsidiary of a publicly listed company.

The new company required a fresh image and we became Micos Inc. The name should have been Micos Computer Systems Limited, but since we also operated in the French- Canadian province of Quebec, that would have required two names, English and French. The shorter name of Micos Inc. could not be translated, so could be used in both jurisdictions. That's the reality of doing nationwide business in this officially bilingual land.

I made frequent trips to New York around that time, flying to La Guardia airport and driving through the Bronx to the town of Elmsford, where MCS was based. Elmsford's only other claim to fame was that David Berkowitz, the serial killer known as Son of Sam, had worked at the factory next to MCS.

On one trip to MCS, I took along a reseller of ours, named Bud, who happened to be a private aircraft pilot. I myself was learning to fly and I had taken a couple of flights with Bud at his flying club in King City. We decided to charter an old twin-engine aircraft from Buttonville Airport, just outside of Toronto. Bud's son was an airline pilot for Air Canada and, since it was his day off, he offered to come along with us. The aircraft we had chartered had seen a hard life and did not foster confidence, but since the weather was beautiful and we planned to be back before dark, there was no reason to worry. The flight to New York went without incident but, upon arrival at Westchester Airport, I can remember feeling distinctly inferior as we taxied past rows of gleaming corporate jets. Westchester must hold the record as a base for that type of aircraft.

Our business meeting at MCS went well and we were able to take off from Westchester by late afternoon; it was summer and there was plenty of daylight left for our return to Buttonville. Since I was learning to fly, I was given the chance to fly in the right-hand seat and took over the controls for part of the flight. What we hadn't reckoned with was a change in the weather; a line of thunderstorms was moving up toward Lake Ontario. Not having a pressurised cabin, we could not fly over thunder clouds that towered 25,000 feet. We had to divert around the storms and this added hours to our journey. By the time we neared Toronto, Buttonville Airport was closed and we were diverted to Toronto International Airport. Air traffic control directed us to change course somewhere above the south shore of Lake Ontario, until we could join the line of 747s, DC8s and other large aircraft coming in for a landing. Now we were glad we had a professional pilot from Air Canada at the controls.

The scene outside the aircraft was humbling but majestic. We were flying at an altitude of 10,000 feet, over low, patchy clouds and caught an occasional glimpse of the ground. It looked as though we were flying inside a deep canyon, surrounded by huge storm clouds towering 15,000 feet above us, with their tops still illuminated by the setting sun. But in the bowels of the dark clouds on either side of the aircraft there were flashes of lightning. Occasionally, amid breaks in the "canyon walls" we spotted a much larger aircraft flying above us. The tension in the cockpit intensified.

We would now be landing in the dark under an extremely low ceiling so it became an instrument approach. I braced a hand against the cabin ceiling to stop being tossed around by the turbulence. Rain was streaming across the front window and, apart from the lightning flashes, it was completely black outside.

Suddenly we realised that most of our instrument lights did not work. No matter how good a pilot is, he or she cannot land using an instrument approach if half the instruments are not visible. We found a rechargeable flashlight in the cabin, but when I switched it on, it quickly discharged and died. I was still a smoker in those days and used my cigarette lighter to illuminate the altimeter and call out the altitude readings for the pilot. Once in a while, he would ask me to check other instruments. We kept looking out the window trying to spot the ground, which was coming up fast. The pilot was not confident that the instrument landing system was accurately calibrated so we could be several hundred yards on either side of the runway.

The altimeter was showing us dangerously close to the ground. All of a sudden, some factory roof tops came into view and immediately I recognised that we were crossing Dixie Road, very close to our office. Having driven on that road daily for the past eight years and regularly flying over it on commercial flights, I knew instinctively that we were off track for the runway, but I knew which way the pilot had to turn. He banked the aircraft to the left and we caught sight of the runway lights. The pilot lined up the aircraft and made a perfect landing. Today, our cigarette packs shout the health warning, "Smoking Kills" but on that night, it was a case of, "Smoking Saves Lives."

I continued to run Micos Inc. with few changes needed, except that I was inundated with paperwork to satisfy U.S.

corporate regulations and also made frequent trips to New York for meetings with my new bosses at MCS. They were agreeable fellows but typically parochial Americans who had little idea of the market opportunities outside the United States. Micos was their only foreign subsidiary, thus they automatically thought of me whenever they had enquiries from overseas. One such case was the Japanese trading company, Marubeni Corporation. When Marubeni suggested that MCS appoint someone to take care of their account, my boss raised the issue at a meeting and proposed me for that role:

"Well, John is the only person we have doing business internationally; so, why don't we have him take care of them?"

That question signalled my anointment as "International Sales Manager" for MCS. Wasting no time, I quickly bought a couple of books on doing business in Japan and prepared to host my first visitor. My guest, Takeshi Murakami, would fly directly to Toronto where I would host him for a couple of days and together we would go to New York to visit MCS. I had heard that an earlier visitor from Marubeni had taken offense at the lack of social interaction with MCS employees. In retaliation, when an MCS computer programmer went to Tokyo to visit Marubeni, he was left to make his own way from his hotel to the Marubeni offices and back, and spent his evenings alone in the hotel.

I was certainly not going to repeat that social mistake. I did not let Murakami-san out of my sight. We exchanged gifts, dined and drank together, and he returned to Tokyo with nothing but positive feelings about our business relationship. Soon after, when I made my first visit to Tokyo, the hospitality was returned in spades. I was in Tokyo for a week and they assigned someone to take me out every single night. By week's end, I was exhausted but the new business relationship was now on firm foundations. On subsequent visits to Tokyo, I was received like an old friend and my Marubeni comrades delighted in taking me to their favourite bars and chuckling at my attempts to entertain them with karaoke.

My international role covered the Pacific-Rim countries and Asia. Had MCS continued with this foreign initiative, we would have had several more partners like the Marubeni Corporation. After establishing the ties with Marubeni, we travelled with the U.S. Department of Commerce and exhibited at a trade show in Taiwan. This led to the appointment of the Tatung Company, one of the largest industrial companies in Taiwan, as our distributor. Tatung purchased our display system right off the exhibition floor and we expected to sell many more systems through this company. But, in hindsight, I am sure Tatung purchased our Micos system—and probably many other competing systems—as part of a plan to evaluate the market potential of their own product. This was two years before the first IBM PC appeared on the market; today, Tatung is one of the biggest suppliers of PCs to the North American market. My sole memento from that Tatung transaction is a photograph of me with Chairman W.S. Lin, seated between the American and Taiwanese flags and signing an agreement. Lin's father, and previous chairman, was T.S. Lin, a colleague of Taiwan's founder, President Chiang Kai-shek.

I also visited India and Australia to discuss business opportunities for MCS. In India, I met with Ratan Tata, the head of India's largest industrial conglomerate and the distributor for IBM. Since then, India has undergone such sweeping economic development, that my being able to get an appointment with Mr. Tata seems extraordinary. Today, he owns a vast range of companies, which includes Jaguar and Land Rover. Networking for business opportunities with Ratan Tata would be like sitting down for talks with Bill Gates.

Australia was different. It was the only country where I found any operating system software to compete with Micos and, although our product was probably superior, I could not get a buyer to adopt our software. As I later observed many times over, Australia's geographic isolation confirmed the old truism: Necessity is the mother of invention. Buying and adapting an American-made solution was too difficult; it was easier to develop one locally.

Australia made a profound impression on me. I found it culturally similar to England, with aspects of language and humour that I yearned for, but was deprived of, in Canada. Yet, Australia lacked those characteristics that made me leave England, and it was clearly influenced by American values, so I felt at home. Little did I realise then that, within a few years, I would be calling it home. On a second trip to Australia, our company set up an exhibit, courtesy of the U.S. Department of Commerce, and this gave me a chance to meet many of the leaders in the computer business.

I struck a friendship with the exhibitor in the stand next to ours. He would one day play a key role in my future. This was Barry de Ferranti, a pioneer in the Australian computer establishment, and at this show he was promoting a "Who's Who" of the industry. I made a note that, if someone needed information, Barry was the man to contact. There always are choices in the journey of life and the chosen path will determine the ultimate destination. Every decision is a potential alteration of course, with known and unknown consequences. Meeting Barry would prove very significant in shaping the outcome of my life's journey, although at the time I couldn't possibly have guessed this.

The hospitality I received from industry colleagues during my Australian visits was fantastic. I would have loved the chance to visit Australia more often, or even move there right away, but my life back in Canada was too complicated and demanding.

Signing the distribution agreement between MCS Inc and the Tatung Company in Taiwan.

CHAPTER 10

*

PRIVATE LIFE UPHEAVALS

BY THE END OF the 1970s, I had been involved in a whirlwind of business activity and, to some extent, had neglected my home life. Children are usually fine in such circumstances because they easily accept that Daddy has to travel and there are always the benefits of travel stories to be told and little souvenirs brought home. Whenever possible, they would be included in trips added to the start or finish of a business trip, such as the time I rented a Winnebago motor home in Atlanta and drove the kids around Florida.

While touring Florida, I was driving the Winnebago along Daytona Beach. This 30-foot behemoth was so easy to drive, and I was so relaxed as I cruised the beach, that I forgot about the air conditioning unit on the roof as I drove under one of Daytona's piers. We were crawling along at about 10 miles per hour, then came to a sudden stop, firmly wedged under the pier. A painter was working on a ladder, close to where we hit, and he was quite upset that I had almost knocked him off his perch. The Winnebago would not budge, either forward or back. A crowd gathered and was obviously amused by this Clark Griswold-like performance. One of the onlookers suggested letting air out of the tires and it worked. I backed the motor home out of the pier's vice-like grip. No damage was done to the vehicle but the freshly painted pier had a gouge in it's woodwork but no structural damage. The structural damage that did occur was purely to my ego.

Marriage partners are different in this respect, and unless they have their own interests and pursuits to fill their lives, an entrepreneurial career—where the spouse is frequently absent from home and constantly focused on non-family challenges—can be fatal to a marriage. My business activity may have been a catalyst, but the real reason for our marriage breakdown was the personal development I had gone through and the self-realisation it had created. May and I had grown apart, over the years; other than our children, we seemed to have very little in common. I addressed the problem as though it were another business issue that had to be solved, which was ridiculous and probably makes a statement about my personality.

We discussed our relationship with our family doctor, who suggested that May apply to attend university as a means of creating another interest in her life. That was basically a good idea, but perhaps too big a step to take at one time. May found the studies difficult and the frustration only added another problem in her mind. The doctor also suggested going to a marriage counsellor, which we did, and I found the regular sessions with the counsellor to be of great value. His professional advice took me from analysing the problem like some business issue, to a new world of interpreting feelings and emotions.

For me, this was definitely a new learning experience and one that clarified a lot of issues in my head. He opened my mind to accepting the idea of not being married, yet still maintaining a relationship for the benefit of our children. I might have failed at this particular marriage, but my ex-wife and I could continue to lead positive and enjoyable lives. May did not see it the same way and, for some years, she blamed the marriage counsellor for our break up. This was unfortunate because we all could have benefitted from further counselling after May and I had separated.

The result was that I made the decision to go out on my own, leaving my wife the family house and agreeing to have joint custody of our children, although their primary home was to be with their mother. Both of us were in our late thirties, having been married for sixteen years, and the children were aged 13, 11 and 7. This was an extremely upsetting time for the kids, although I am sure the situation could have been handled better if some of the bitterness between Mum and Dad had not existed. The children certainly could not be blamed for the split up, but I know they felt somehow responsible. In hindsight, I suppose we were typical of many thousands of marriage breakdowns.

Is marital discord or a marriage breakdown an occupational hazard for all entrepreneurs? I'm not sure, but I'm tempted to think that entrepreneurial activities can be harmful to your relationships. I do know that my life experiences, especially during my thirties, transformed me through a developmental process; and this gradual metamorphosis might well have led to the failure of our marriage. I have seen this happen to a lot of married colleagues after they have experienced a similar process of personal development, over a period of years.

Outside my business life, the Association of Kinsmen continued to throw challenges my way. During the early-1980s, I travelled to East Africa as a guest of Round Table, sister organisation to Kinsmen. Four of us Kinsmen members made the trip, paying only our own airfares, while the local Round Table clubs in Ethiopia, Kenya and Tanzania furnished our accommodation in members' homes, supplied the land-based transportation and covered our attendance at their national convention in Mombasa. What a way to see Africa, I thought, and discover how people lived in those countries. I was planning to go alone but, at the last minute, Evi, an Air Canada flight attendant friend of mine, asked whether she could join me if she paid her own way.

The plan was to fly to London, then catch an Ethiopian Airlines flight, via Asmara, to Addis Ababa, the Ethiopian capital. At the last moment, we were alerted to cancel the Ethiopian segment of the trip because an insurrection had flared up there, against the communist government. Evi and I decided to leave the trip as planned and find a Western hotel in Addis Ababa when we arrived. It was a tense time to visit Ethiopia but we were admitted into the country since we held onward tickets to Tanzania and had a reservation at the Hilton Hotel.

Walking through the city was no ordinary tourist excursion. At the former palace of deposed King Haile Selassie, I was waved on at gunpoint by soldiers and told not to take photographs. Later in the day, we met our hotel's tennis pro, a former long-distance runner on the Ethiopian team at the 1980 Moscow Olympics. He joined us for lunch at a traditional Ethiopian restaurant, where we sampled a local—but unidentifiable—meat by tearing off a piece of flat bread, spread out like a table cloth, and scooping up the meat with it. Soon, he would be setting off on a two-day trek to his village, where he was marrying a 12-year-old bride arranged by his family. He explained that, after the wedding ceremony, he would take his bride inside their hut, consummate the marriage and, to "prove" that she was a virgin, he would spill chicken blood on a bed cloth to be shown to the guests expectantly waiting outside.

Our next stop was Arusha, in Tanzania, not far from the base of Mount Kilimanjaro, Africa's highest peak. This time, we were met by our hosts and attended the first of many Round Table meetings. Members were much like Kinsmen, young men under 40 and most of them business or professional people. They were a mixture mostly of Indians, some Africans, and a few Europeans. During the first few days, we were taken to Tanzania's signature game parks—Lake Manyara and Ngorongoro Crater. Given the sad state of Tanzania's economy at the time, accommodation would be quite unlike anything I was accustomed to. We took our own toilet rolls and light bulbs, as these were perennially in short supply. The only alcohol available was a local beer, and our hosts urged us not to fret about the lack of choice because every bottle of beer was different.

The scenery and wildlife were spectacular and this experience was intensified because we encountered no other tourists and were able to get very close to the animals. Imagine standing up in an open-top Volkswagen Kombi minibus which has parked under a tree, and getting so close to a pride of lions resting in its shade, that you can hear them panting. Throughout the three-day safari, we had similarly exhilarating approaches to Tanzania's big game—rhinos, hippopotami, cheetahs and elephants.

We returned to Arusha for a night, then began a 435-km drive on dirt roads to the Indian Ocean coast and the town of Tanga. The Round Table members in Arusha would drive us halfway to the coast, and Tanga members would meet us at a pre-arranged point to drive us from there. But our car had a flat tire and a spare could not be found anywhere in town. So, they put us into a taxi and sent us to rendezvous with the Tanga members, somewhere in the bush. The taxi driver got the incorrect rendezvous point and, with no telephone and a driver who spoke no English, we were stuck. Several hours passed. I began to communicate with the driver in sign language and drew a map on the ground with a stick, to indicate that we wanted him to drive us to Tanga. He had never been that far in his life and was anxious to drive off and return to Arusha. In the end, I used the international language of bribery and with the incentive of a few hundred Tanzanian shillings, he agreed to take us to Tanga.

When we arrived, we had no idea where to go so we got the driver to take us to the police station. The police spoke almost no English, but they allowed us to use the telephone and call our Tanga contact, Hatim Karimjee. Hatim was amazed that we were already in Tanga but was shocked to hear that we were at the police station.

"Don't say anything to the police!" he instructed. "We'll come and get you!"

Apparently, Tanzanians, especially those with an Indian background, are very suspicious of the police. Hatim's family was of Indian descent and once owned some of the largest sisal plantations, before the Communist government confiscated most of these holdings and allowed the family to keep just the most uneconomical property. Hatim later took over these seized estates, now operated by the government, and his company became the largest exporter of sisal and sisal products in Tanzania.

Hatim Karimjee still managed to live like a colonial gentleman and the days we spent with him were the most pleasant of the trip. He showed us his former family home, now all closed and boarded up. His parents had relocated to Spain, leaving Hatim to run the family investments in Tanzania. He took us deep-sea fishing in the Indian Ocean, in his power cruiser, but how he was able to get fuel for it is a mystery.

One of the reasons Round Table invited us to Tanzania was to obtain donations from Kinsmen for various local community projects. We visited several schools for handicapped children and I eventually convinced our Mississauga Kinsmen club to make some small donations. But the Tanzanian government's handling of past donations did give us second thoughts. For instance, the Tanga Club had arranged for Round Table India to donate medical equipment for the local hospital and to send medical teams to perform various target treatments. The moment the Indian teams completed their work and left Tanzania, the government appropriated the donated equipment at the hospital and either sold it or used it in other places. Thus, all the good work of the Round Table was undone.

From Tanga, we flew to the capital, Dar es Salaam, on what was probably the last flight of Tanzanian Airlines. Most of their aircraft had been grounded for lack of parts. I spoke to the Swiss pilot of our aircraft and he told me that the airline had run out of fuel. The pilot had not been paid, so this was his final flight and he was returning to Switzerland.

We took a bus from Dar es Salaam to Kenya, via Tanga, to attend a convention in Mombasa. It was miraculous that we made it to Mombasa, because the bus looked as though it had been driven for several million miles. Along the way, we saw many large vehicles abandoned on the road where they had come to a halt. Tanzania had no tow trucks large enough to haul a bus or truck out of a ditch; where the vehicle was blocking the road, the traffic simply created another track around the blockage. The border with Kenya was officially closed but we had special permission to cross, the "special" part of that permission consisting of bribes paid to the border guards. Kenya was a much more functional country than Tanzania so we discarded our toilet rolls and light bulbs and prepared to see another part of East Africa.

After the convention in Mombasa, we took the train to Nairobi, where we stayed with the first European Africans we had encountered on this trip. From Nairobi, we headed for Mount Kenya, Nakuru, and Kisumu on the shores of Lake Victoria. The lodge at Mount Kenya overlooked a watering hole which attracted a host of wild animals, a nature scene matched only by the spectacle of Lake Nakuru—coloured pink by the presence of hundreds of thousands of flamingos. We returned to Nairobi to catch a flight to London. In true African fashion, I was hit for hundreds of dollars-worth of excess baggage charges, but this was quickly settled with a twenty-dollar bribe to the man who was checking me in.

Toughing It Out

I consider it important to have challenging and interesting activities outside of one's business interests. Of course, a trip such as the one I took to East Africa can lead to fresh opportunities because the people I visited and travelled with were like-minded business people. But there is more to it than that. The example that Hatim Karimjee set for me, in managing and retaining his family's business under such trying circumstances, was an inspirational lesson that I could take home and use to rekindle my motivation.

CHAPTER 11

SHIFTING BUSINESS GEARS

THE COMPUTER INDUSTRY IN the late-1970s was dynamic and ever changing. Companies were formed then disappeared almost overnight and the future of the industry was very hard to gauge. This was still a couple of years before IBM introduced the personal computer and the market battle was between mini-computers from manufacturers like Digital, Data General and Hewlett Packard in one camp, and in the other camp the new micro-computer makers whose machines were based on Intel chips, forerunners to the PCs. In the world of business applications, the mini-computers still had the lion's share of the market.

A few years ago, I visited the Computer History Museum in Mountain View, California and truly grasped how rapidly the industry had been changing during that era. Not only have the two market leaders of the time, DEC and Data General, completely disappeared but significant players like General Automation, Prime Computers, Texas Instruments and Wang Laboratories have long ago left the market for other opportunities. Also at that time, there was an emerging group of micro-computers, favoured by hobbyists, including the Altair, the Commodore 64, the TRS-80 and the Apple II. It was a very difficult time for business survival in the IT industry.

Micos Canada continued to prosper, but MCS made some bad decisions, trying to diversify into manufacturing and into business-specific applications. Had they concentrated instead on what they did best by developing operating system software, they might have been the company that supplied IBM with an operating system, in place of Microsoft. But they did not, and since my fate was tied up inextricably with MCS, I was again forced to be proactive in moulding my future. MCS was headed for Chapter 11, under the bankruptcy laws, and before that happened I needed to reclaim my company. My approach to Bill Doniger, the President of MCS, was accepted enthusiastically since it offered the possibility of a cash injection for MCS which they badly needed. In fact, MCS began selling various parts of the company, including the loss-making manufacturing facility in California and was able to survive for a few more years.

Once again, I began looking for venture capital. Ever since MCS had acquired the company, Micos Canada had grown and remained profitable, so the selling price was going to be much higher than the price MCS had paid when they bought the company. But MCS were rather desperate sellers. My own resources were very much depleted, since going through my divorce, and my only investment—my shares in MCS—were still in escrow and very much reduced in value.

This time around, it seemed to me that raising a consortium of investors might be the most effective way of purchasing Micos Canada and it would leave me with a healthy investment, but regrettably not under my control. One of my employees was willing to invest $40,000 and a friend from The Kinsmen Club would also invest the same amount. My lawyer in Toronto was a partner in a large Bay Street law firm and wanted to make an investment as well; he also had partners and clients who would do the same. Toronto's Bay Street is the Wall Street of Canada. Occasionally, I met at the Cambridge Club with my lawyer and some of these potential investors—a group that I later came to call the Bay Street Mafia.

With investors such as these, expectations of growth and what will be achieved are quite often unrealistic. They get the impression that investing in a computer company will yield a rapid increase in the value of their investment, for a short-term capital gain. This was the same investment fervour that, years later, would drive the "dot com" boom of the late-1990s. In actual fact, Micos Canada, as a financially healthy distributor of computer hardware and software, represented a good long-term investment.

The buy-back of Micos Canada was successful and I continued building the company while reporting to a board of directors, consisting largely of the Bay Street Mafioso. With the loss of George Coupar and Jim Tomkins to other companies, I needed to add to my management team. I promoted an engineer to George's former position and supported his project to integrate a business-friendly version of a new operating system called UNIX. It's ironic that, today, I work on Apple Macintosh computers whose OS-X software is based on UNIX. We might have succeeded with that project 25 years before Apple did it. To replace Jim Tomkins, I recruited Wayne Thompson, our former Data General salesman, and made him Vice President of Sales. I also appointed an accountant with an MBA, as our financial controller.

My overseas travels came to an end. Instead, travel across Canada became the norm. We had offices in Vancouver, Edmonton, Toronto and Montreal so I would have been amassing frequent flyer points if they had loyalty programs like that, in 1980. My social life was not going anywhere at this time. I became less involved with Kinsmen after the breakdown of my marriage. The Kinsmen Club of Mississauga was a married man's club and my ex-wife was President of the Club's women's auxiliary, in the year we split up, so she was still very friendly with the wives of other Kinsmen. In effect, she got custody of my friends. Thus, my socializing was limited to business associates and, for a casual drink after work, I would look to the single guys who worked for Micos. Frank Delling was one of these.

Frank was a German migrant to Canada. Having recently broken up with his partner, he and I were looking for any excuse to go out on the town. We did so regularly, checking out most of Toronto's singles bars and, in keeping with the spirit of those places, remaining definitely single. Another colleague who was suited to the single bars was Sergius, whose dark skin and black hair allowed him to develop an impressive afro haircut. The single life was short-lived for Sergius, though, and soon I was attending his wedding. Upon catching up with him, not too long ago, the afro had been transformed into a shiny dome.

Frank and a fellow who worked at Micos lived next door to two single girls, Jeanne and Colleen. Both girls grew up in other parts of Canada and moved to Toronto after they had met while backpacking around Europe. In June, 1981, the girls hosted a party and I was dragged along as one of the few eligible bachelors. It turned out to be a very auspicious party for me: within two years, and precisely on the opposite side of the Planet from Toronto, Colleen and I got married. Life was spinning very fast indeed.

When Colleen and I started dating, we compared notes and swapped stories about our separate travels. She recounted her hostelling experiences around Europe, working in the City of London, and illegally tending an American bar in Greece. I described my adventures in Africa and visits to India, Japan and particularly Australia, the country that she and Jeanne planned to visit next.

By now, Canada's economy had slid into a recession. With a slowdown in economic activity, record-high interest rates, and government-imposed wage and price controls, the management team at Micos Canada was faced with significant challenges. All of our resellers were reporting sales figures well below what they had projected twelve months earlier and the computer industry, in general, was struggling. For the financial year 1981, our sales at Micos totalled $3.5 million, up from $3.1 million in the previous year and we had stayed profitable (in today's dollars, that sales figure would be three to four times as much). Our shareholders, however, had unreasonably high expectations as to what could be achieved by Micos. I had misread the degree to which the shareholders and directors understood the real situation and, unknown to me at the time, I was being undermined from inside the company.

On January 19, 1982, I showed up at the boardroom on 390 Bay Street, in Toronto, for my regular monthly meeting with Chairman of the Board Paul Palmer and my solicitor, John Gilfillan, who was the company secretary. January in Toronto is always cold but not as cold as the atmosphere in the room, that morning. There was a noticeable lack of pleasantries and the Chairman came straight to the point. Because Micos had not met the year-to-date sales and profit targets, the Board was voting to terminate my employment as President of the company.

I could not fathom why I was being fired. This was my company and I had created it! Palmer explained that I could take the matter to the shareholders, but he had already canvassed the investors who he had brought into the syndicate. Their votes would outweigh the votes I held, by virtue of my own investment and that of the shareholders I had brought in. They had it all sown up. No consideration was given to the fact that we were still growing and making profits. There was no discussion that took into account the shares that I owned in Micos. There was no opportunity for any discussion at all. They had made their decision and I was out. I knew, then, that I would first have to consult an independent legal source, now that my own solicitor was party to the action against me.

As I left the boardroom, I found Wayne Thompson waiting in the reception area and about to enter the boardroom. Suddenly, the whole plot fell into place. I had recruited a Trojan Horse by hiring and appointing Wayne Thompson as Vice President, and he had been working on Palmer and Gilfillan to replace me and install himself as President. A cascade of recent events and meetings involving Thompson flooded into my mind and completed the picture of what he had been up to and why. His behaviours should have raised my suspicions, but my generally trusting nature had predisposed me to overlook them. This game had been playing out for some time but I didn't have a clue it was taking place.

I left the building and trudged through the snow, making my way down the street to Peter's Backyard, a bar that Colleen and I frequented in the same building where she worked. I called Colleen from the pay phone and asked her to meet me in the bar downstairs. Then I ordered something really strong—a double Rusty Nail. When Colleen showed up I told her that her new boyfriend was now unemployed and no longer ran his own company. She bathed and rinsed me in moral support and helped me pull myself together. With her encouragement, I was going to fight this injustice.

Next day, I called a law firm specialising in wrongful dismissal cases and went to see them. Various courses of legal action were open to me, all of them potentially costly, but we agreed to take action for wrongful dismissal and to raise the matter of Gilfillan's apparent conflict of interest as my solicitor.

The wheels of legal action turn slowly, but my new lawyer hoped to get some discussions going with Palmer and Gilfillan, based on the filing of our claim for wrongful dismissal. In the meantime, I could not visit our offices and the Micos employees had been warned by Wayne Thompson not to speak with me. We had about fifty employees at the time, and I was very appreciative that more than half of them ignored their new boss's instructions and called me with thanks and words of encouragement. The Montreal office had a ski weekend coming up at Grey Rocks, which Colleen and I had planned to attend, and we decided to go despite what had happened. It turned out to be a great weekend and the many staff members who came were completely supportive of me and sympathetic about my dismissal. Wayne Thompson did not show up, otherwise he would have observed the serious morale problem facing him in his new position. He might also have had a nasty accident on the ski slopes.

While I waited for the outcome of the legal battle, I should mention that, after I had migrated to Australia some years later, I was contacted by Gilfillan and offered a first class return trip from Australia to Canada, to testify against Thompson because Micos had fired him and were suing him over another matter. They eventually settled out of court so I didn't make that trip, but it was somewhat reassuring to hear that they regretted their action against me.

CHAPTER 12

※

OPTIONS GALORE

THE NEXT FEW WEEKS were spent brainstorming my options for the future. My first task was to find another job and I contacted everyone in my network to see who might have an opening for someone with my experience. The situation looked grim. The economic downturn in Canada had hit the computer industry particularly hard and there were almost no jobs advertised for someone in my position. The general manager of one of my former resellers had moved to San Francisco and he suggested I would easily find a position there, but that didn't address the problem of getting a work visa for the USA. I also had discussions with MCS about a job in America and the work visa barrier was the same.

The talks with my lawyer continued and he was positive I would receive an offer of a pay-out for my wrongful dismissal and my shares. That prospect filled my head with images of a big cash injection and, along with Colleen and Jeanne, I explored the idea of buying a boat and sailing around the world. An Australian friend and business colleague was building a boat with the intention of sailing to Australia and the girls and I spent hours listening to his plans and adapting them to our sailing idea. We started taking sailing courses, visited boat yards, and I daydreamed about taking off and sailing away from my problems. This was certainly not an example of toughing it out.

Before long, reality hit hard when I realised that my pay-out would be nowhere near the amount needed to fulfil this dream and meet my commitment to support my children. I returned to the grind of printing my resume and visiting employment agencies in the hunt for a job. But there were absolutely no jobs advertised anywhere in Canada that I could realistically apply for. I continued to approach U.S. companies but I could not convince any prospective employer to make me an offer. For most, it was easier to hire a local employee and avoid the paperwork involved in obtaining a work visa for me.

Colleen was a pillar of support during the following three months. She worked in the travel industry and, at one of the promotional events put on by airlines and tour companies, she won a trip for two to Antigua, in the West Indies. I was quick to point out my availability as a travel companion and she agreed to take me. Thus, within three months of getting fired from my job, I was preparing for a Caribbean holiday.

Two weeks before leaving for Antigua, I picked up an Australian newspaper at one of the specialty shops in Toronto and, to my utter amazement, there were pages and pages of job advertisements in the computer industry. I had the Tuesday issue of The Australian, which regularly features the IT industry. The job ad that caught my eye was a company whose managing director, Paul Wood, I had met when visiting Australia. I rummaged through my business cards and, that evening, placed a call to Paul Wood. He told me there was a serious shortage of experienced people throughout the computer industry and I could easily get a job and a work visa. In fact, he was willing to consider me for a position in his company if I could get to Australia for an interview. Could he see me in three to four weeks, I asked. Paul checked his calendar and pencilled an appointment with me in the second week of May.

I spent the next two weeks assiduously studying the Australian computer industry and focusing my search on Sydney. I wrote letters to likely employers and booked flights for a two-week stay in Sydney. As well, I lined up a list of prospects that I would be telephoning, after returning from Antigua. It felt good to be working once again on something positive.

The Antiguan getaway was a splendidly relaxing week. But our departure on the free flight with British West Indian Airlines was also a splendid lesson on the airline's habit of overbooking in order to ensure that every seat had a bum in it. Since we held promotional tickets, the aircraft's purser decided we were fair game for removal in order to solve the overbooking problem. He came down the aisle and said,

"Hey, mon! You gotta off. We got another flight next week. We'll get you back then."

Our tickets clearly stated that we were in a Must Ride category, meaning that we could not be bumped off this flight, so we stood our ground.

"No way," I replied. "We have Must Ride tickets."

"It don't matter, mon," he insisted. "You gotta get off."

He went away and came back to report that the aircraft's captain wanted us to get off the plane. After all I had gone through recently, in Canada, I had no intention of getting stuck in the Caribbean, when a pile of work was awaiting me, in preparation for my trip to Australia. Eventually, a family of four was persuaded to share two seats and two passengers were put into flight attendant jump seats, so we could take off.

When I got back to Toronto, there was a message to ring Barry de Ferranti, in Australia. I had written to him to ask about opportunities for me in Sydney. I returned his phone call and he confirmed what Paul Wood had said: there were good job prospects for me in Australia. We arranged to meet when I got to Sydney.

It is Friday, 7 May, 1982. I board a jet at Toronto International Airport—today, the world's 18th busiest airport and renamed Lester B. Pearson International Airport—and fly halfway around the world to Sydney. I cross the Date Line, which puts me into Sydney on Sunday morning, May 9. The calendar date, Saturday, May 8, 1982, does not exist in my life. I have never lived through this day.

I met with Barry that night and had several interviews lined up for the first few days of the week ahead—and lots of other people to call. It was simply mind-boggling that, having been unable to get a single interview in Canada throughout three months of job hunting, I would be averaging two interviews a day, for the next ten working days of my time in Australia. What a difference place and time can make!

Barry de Ferranti explained that he was working on behalf of a client who might need someone like me; he would get back to me on this. In the meantime, I got through first interviews with Systems Technology and Data General and was asked to return for second interviews the following week. On Friday, Barry confirmed that his client, a company named Eracom, was interested in me and was located on the Gold Coast. My first reaction was that I didn't want to go to Africa. I then found out that the city of Gold Coast was the recently renamed municipality south of Brisbane, the State of Queensland's capital. Eracom would book me a flight to Gold Coast and I would meet the company owner on the last day of my Australian visit. Because I was fairly confident I would find a job in Sydney, I hesitated to go for this interview but, in the end, made the trip to Queensland.

It was a beautiful day when I arrived on the shores of the Coral Sea in the South Pacific, at the eastern tip of Australia. Eracom had booked me into the Chevron Hotel, the Gold Coast's finest hotel at the time. I took a stroll around the Surfers Paradise neighbourhood where the hotel stood and thought, I don't care what the job is; I'm taking it. This little corner of the globe has pristine beaches of golden-white sand and, right under my feet, an unbroken stretch of ocean beach, 17 kilometres long. The climate is temperate-perfect and plants bloom year-round; a 30-minute drive inland via winding, scenic roads brings one into the Hinterland, a lush subtropical rainforest carpeting a 2,000-foot-high plateau and embracing four national parks. Dotting the Hinterland are quaint little townships.

My lesson from this: when interviewing prospective employees, make a splendid first impression and they will do anything to work for you.

Eracom was established in Canberra, Australia's national capital, and recently had been purchased by Bruce Small, one of the Gold Coast's most recognised land developers. Bruce's late father was Sir Bruce Small, former Mayor of Gold Coast, and often referred to as the father of the Gold Coast. Bruce Small Junior was better known by his nickname, Kelly. Having lived in his father's shadow for years, Kelly was determined to make his own mark by attracting information technology companies like Eracom to the Gold Coast. He even had a name for this promising development: Silicon Paradise.

Eracom had several products in various stages of development. The company had produced an Intel-based personal computer called the ERA50, which ran on the CP/M operating system, and broke new ground a year before IBM introduced its famous Personal Computer that revolutionised computing. They also had developed a multi-user version of the computer, the ERA80, which had the potential of replacing minicomputer systems like MICOS. Users at that time found it hard to understand the capability of the PC, and we certainly had no inkling of the possibilities, once PCs would be networked together.

Another product under development at Eracom was an encryption feature that would secure data within the computer, as well as on storage media, by scrambling the information according to an encryption algorithm. This work was very unique at the time and the company was finding it difficult to persuade users of the need for this type of security. Eracom was very much ahead of its time.

Eight of the company's employees had moved to the Gold Coast, from Canberra, and they were all very much involved in research and development. Among them were two nuclear physicists, including the company's founder, Dr. Bill Caelli. Eracom was more like a university laboratory than a commercial operation. With such a strong product development background, they needed a marketing person. And since Kelly Small's vision included exporting to the United States, they were looking for a marketing person with North American experience. I was their man.

Kelly took me on a short tour of the office/development facilities where Eracom was temporarily located and later invited me to his palatial home on the Nerang River. This was an experience in itself. The house was located on a bend in the river, a spectacular site and one of the landmarks shown to tourists taking a boat tour on the river. The tour guides giving the commentary would say things like, "Even the dogs have air conditioned bedrooms and flush toilets." The latter part was not true.

When the day ended, we agreed that I would move to the Gold Coast as soon as I could get an immigration visa under Eracom's sponsorship. I was to be the new General Manager of Eracom. In the meantime, I would carry out some work for Eracom in America, doing market research and attending the National Computer Conference, in Houston, with Barry de Ferranti. I also arranged to meet Kelly Small, in Los Angeles, and assist him with a consulting relationship he had formed to develop business for Eracom.

I flew back to Sydney, that night, feeling light enough to fly without an aircraft. Not only had I achieved what I had set out to do on this trip, I had landed a great job in the best place in Australia. The next day, I flew home to Canada and celebrated with Colleen. She and Jeanne began planning for their trip down under. Our relationship and my business career were rapidly, inexorably converging.

My next challenge was a delicate one—explaining to my children that I was moving to the other side of the world. I had come to accept this planned move as a rational decision and likened it to being in the Air Force and being posted overseas. Thousands of fathers were in that position and maintained healthy relationships with their children. I had the added benefit that Eracom wanted to develop export sales to North America, so I saw myself traveling to Canada several times a year.

I took the kids out to dinner and broke the news to them. I don't recall any major disappointment on their part; my optimism about the move must have rubbed off. I told them what a great place the Gold Coast is and that they would be visiting me during their holidays, the following year. I pointed out that we would need to write letters to each other, and this is exactly what we ended up doing. I still have some of those letters. I wonder how many of today's traveling fathers will keep the e-mails and text messages they received from their children. Very few, is my guess. The loss of letter-writing habits and skills is one of the outcomes of a person's enslavement to the Internet.

Now, I was busy again but brooding over how long it would take the Australian Government to process my visa application. Two weeks later, I was flying to Houston to join Barry de Ferranti at the National Computer Conference and evaluate products that would compete with Eracom's innovations. A month later, I went to California to meet Eracom's Dr. Bill Caelli and visit the new workstation company, Sun Microsystems, in Santa Clara, the company formed as a spin off from Stanford University. We had talks with the founders of a company that became the leader in computer servers and workstations and which was sold, in 2009, to Oracle for US$7.4 billion.

After our meetings in Silicon Valley, I went to meet Kelly Small in Los Angeles. Kelly wanted me to check on the progress of an

Australian marketing consultant he had hired to develop export opportunities for Eracom. He had a justifiable suspicion that the consultant was acting entirely in self-interest and neglecting Eracom matters. Kelly had come to shut down an Eracom bank account and stop any further siphoning of Eracom's funds.

We arrived at the bank just in time. The consultant's girlfriend was waiting in line to withdraw all the funds from the Eracom account and the consultant was nowhere to be found. I realised then that my boss-to-be was a trusting and well meaning person and this made him quite vulnerable to slick sales pitches. Much later, I discovered that all of the expenses incurred in retaining this consultant were eligible for subsidy under the Australian government's Export Development Grant, which covered expenditures up to $100,000 annually. Eracom was eligible for the maximum subsidy.

Now, however, I was looking for another windfall from the Australian government—a permanent residency visa. The application was put through as an urgent employment need by my sponsor; it was approved two months later.

CHAPTER 13

*

CHANGING CONTINENTS

ON AUGUST 8, 1982, I arrived in Australia with a residence visa to take up my new job on the Gold Coast. But I did have mixed feelings about this move. The Gold Coast was a wonderful place to live but the computer industry was non-existent and the company I was joining was, with the exception of Bill Caelli, staffed by people who lacked experience in the mainstream industry. The owner had only a hazy idea of where he wanted to take the company and I would have no colleagues from other local IT companies with which to network. The company had an odd of mix of products which did not complement each other well, making it difficult to identify a focus for the company's future. On top of all this, I had to avoid being seen as the know-it-all who came from America (not many Aussies could tell the difference between a Canadian and an American) to tell them how things should be done. I didn't even have an office at the company. They worked out of an old converted house which was mainly a workshop and store room. I was given an office at Bruce Small Enterprises, which was the head office of Kelly Small's land development company.

The first thing I noticed was how politically well connected Kelly Small was. Within a few weeks of my arrival, we organised a launch of the ERA-50 personal computer at one of Brisbane's top hotels and the function included the Premier of the State of Queensland, Sir Joh Bjelke-Petersen. Shortly afterward, I was surprised to find the entire Queensland cabinet holding a meeting in Kelly Small's office, complete with the press corps waiting outside. Being a newcomer to Queensland and not knowing who was who in State politics, this kind of event did not impress me at the time. It became a typical experience for me during my time at Eracom. I had landed on my feet next to an extremely well-connected family, in a place that was going through amazing changes. Twenty years on, those transformations are persisting at an accelerating pace. When I first arrived, Gold Coast's population was less than 100,000; now it has passed the half-million mark.

My first task was to determine a direction for Eracom. In this, I had a lot of support from Barry de Ferranti and from the market research company run by Kelly's uncle, Frank Small, in Sydney. We analysed Eracom's strengths and pretty soon determined that we should capitalise on Bill Caelli's expertise and the features he had built into the ERA-50. Our focus would be a unique capability of encrypting data for security purposes and our goal to become the experts in data-systems security. We plugged the ERA-50 as the only computer which guaranteed absolute security of the data stored on the hard disk and we positioned our company as the specialists in making any information secure, anywhere. A graphic design company came up with a James Bond image for our promotional strategy tied to the corporate slogan, "The key to data systems security." I was enthusiastic about the whole thing because it meant having something different to sell in North America.

Kelly Small purchased a new building to bring the company together and finally I had my own office. The ERA-50 sold well to government departments, boosted by the "Buy Australian" policy adopted in the early-1980s. We held an opening ceremony for the new building and Kelly Small's political connections surfaced once again when Andrew Peacock, the Federal Minister for Industry and Commerce, attended. When a picture of Andrew Peacock and me was published in a national newspaper, I was surprised when people noticed and commented on it; my knowledge of Australian politics was close to zero. I learned that Andrew Peacock's government was defeated three months later and he was elected Leader of the Opposition.

We exhibited at all the local computer shows and worked with the Australian government to display our products at the National Computer Conference, in Las Vegas, and the Canadian Computer Conference, in Toronto. The response was positive but not decisive, as often the promotion of new ideas can be. "What a good idea that is!" is the typical reaction from potential customers, but the orders are a long time coming. We signed up a California company to work with us and they found the same experience after we had returned to Australia. They wrote, "Eracom has some fantastic security products and we will be sure to use them in the future." But this future was somewhat undetermined.

The Canadian Computer Conference had a positive result for us, but even this did not become apparent until much later. I met with John Knorr, the computer salesman to whom I had earlier rented some storage space after I had started Integrant, in 1974. He had expanded his business and was selling North American equipment in the European market, in particular Russia. He had made a killing selling computer terminals to the Russians for the Moscow Olympics, somehow getting around the American embargo on those products. He was delighted to see me again and was enthusiastic about selling our security systems. I had to be very firm about not selling to Russia. We used an encryption chip that was controlled by the US Department of Defence and they were strict enough about how it was used in Australia, let alone allowing it to be used in systems shipped behind the Iron Curtain. But John Knorr's eyes lit up at the possible challenge of selling it to the Russians and, if successful, the high price he could guarantee for his efforts.

Our breakthrough in Australian sales of our security products came from the Australia New Zealand Banking Group (ANZ Bank). They wanted us to manufacture a secure hardware device in order to decrypt PIN numbers from credit cards. The ANZ Bank was concerned that their existing method of decrypting PINs through software on computers could be compromised by any smart system software programmer. If they could assign this function to a secure hardware box, the risk would be eliminated. With this goal in mind, we designed and built our first ERA-007 Security Module, complete with James Bond graphics.

But developing and manufacturing a finished commercial product was no easy matter, given the corporate culture at Eracom. Dr. Bill Caelli was more focussed on pure research than on product development and he was forever working on research papers or being interviewed by the media as the country's expert on computer security. He was much more suited to an academic career, and in fact he ended up as a Professor at the Queensland University of Technology. That left me with the option of developing a separate group of Eracom employees whose task would be to produce the finished device for the ANZ Bank. I found a team leader in Eddy Boyes, hired a couple of programmers and a new manufacturing manager, and together we delivered the Security Module to the ANZ Bank, on time and on budget. It was the breakthrough that Eracom desperately needed.

Our new manufacturing manager was a former Group Captain from the Royal Australian Air Force. This was fortuitous because we were required to set up a secure records storage room and assign a person to communicate with the Australian Department of Defence which decided where our encryption chips could be sold. Even as general manager of Eracom, I was not cleared by the Department's Defence Signals Directorate to discuss matters concerning how the chip was used. In fact, at times it seemed as if that part of the Defence Department did not exist. When our manufacturing manager visited the Defence Signals Directorate, in Melbourne, he was incommunicado and no telephone number was given to us where he could be reached.

I did find it ironic to have a former Group Captain working for me, considering that, during my term in the Royal Air Force, I had never met anyone at this high a rank.

Following our success with the ANZ Bank, other financial institutions and credit card providers immediately became interested in Eracom's security module which was, at the time, completely unique in the world. John Knorr arranged to launch our new product in the European market at the 1984 Hannover Fair. His company was a regular exhibitor at Hannover and had clinched the much sought after exhibition space at CEBIT, the computer technology section of the Fair. Once again, we took advantage of Austrade to help us promote our product to financial institutions.

Hannover was a tough show to work, especially after needing to fly the long way around the world, so I could visit my kids in Canada on the way there. Our accommodation was an hour's drive from the fair and the exhibition hours were 9 a.m. to 6 p.m., so it made for a long day without the usual buffer of after-work drinks with all one's industry colleagues. John Knorr ran a bar on his stand, offering his best clients a quick schnapps and sometimes it was impossible to avoid a drink without causing offence. Hannover must be responsible for creating an awful lot of alcoholics.

One night has stayed quite memorable for me, despite the alcoholic haze that permeated the circumstances in my head. We were spending the evening at the Hoffbrau House. I was challenged to conduct the beer hall's brass band and, being an old bandsman from my RAF days, I could not resist the enticement. I led the band through Waltzing Matilda and, as the last few strains of the ditty faded away, I spotted someone across a crowd of some 10,000 people, standing on a table, yelling my name. Life's networking was at work again! It was former President John Collinson from the Kinsmen Club of Mississauga.

Moving halfway around the world meant establishing new friends and business colleagues and the lessons I learned from my days in the Association of Kinsmen were invaluable. I was now too old for a club like Kinsmen but my new accountant was a member of the Mermaid Beach Rotary Club and I quickly became a Rotarian. I count many enjoyable years in the Mermaid Beach and Robina Rotary Clubs and it was only my travel commitments in later years that forced me to give up my membership. It is definitely one of the better organisations for a business person to join for the purpose of networking. Also, the fun and fellowship gained often leads to some valuable charitable activities.

Apart from the lingering sadness of having left my family behind in Canada, my first years in Queensland were truly enjoyable and my challenges were hardly testing. Things seemed to fall into place and much of the credit for that must go to my new boss, Kelly Small. Perhaps he was not tough enough on me but I can certainly say he was hospitable.

Just after I arrived in Australia, Colleen and Jeanne turned up in Sydney, planning to travel around this vast country and catch up with friends they had met while living in Europe. I was quick to suggest that they move to the Gold Coast and since Sydney was still pretty cold at that time of year they didn't need much persuasion. I had rented a house on the Nerang River and there was plenty of room for visiting Canadians which, within weeks, included not only Colleen and Jeanne but also their friends Kim and Kim's rugby playing boyfriend, Lloydie, who were getting together after Kim's travels around India. She had picked up hepatitis in India but you wouldn't know it, given her seemingly boundless energy. Kelly Small welcomed all four of them like long-lost relatives. He insisted that I bring them along to every barbecue and party at his place and his wife, Christa, invited them to join her for tennis lessons at their court whenever I was at work.

Two months after my landing on Australian shores, Brisbane hosted the Commonwealth Games—second, only, in importance to the Olympic Games as an international showcase of sporting prowess—and Kelly took us to the opening and closing ceremonies. I think he enjoyed having a bunch of maple-leaf-clad party animals traveling with him. I was never sure of Christa's feelings in all of this but, in the Aussie vernacular, it was "no worries" with Kelly. He was happy to have us there and showed no concern about paying the bills. We certainly weren't "bludgers" (freeloaders) to him; he was simply so amenable to hosting us.

We went out almost every week to some of Kelly's favourite restaurants. A few of them, Nicolinis in Surfers Paradise and The Loft on Chevron Island, still exist. St. Malos in the suburb of Bundall was another favourite but, since the owner and chef was aged about 70 in those days, his restaurant is no longer in business. We would gather at the Small mansion for drinks before dinner, then head out to a restaurant with an armful of wines selected from Kelly's cellar. Those were the days of no random breath-testing by roadside police. Another Australian bonus was that nearly all Gold Coast restaurants allowed their patrons to bring their own wines to dinner, hence the designation of a BYO (bring your own) eatery. In all this fun, I do recall having to get my new boss off the floor at Nicolinis on one occasion.

Kelly celebrated his 60th birthday while I still had all the Canadians staying with me and this was a majestic affair. It took place at the Small mansion and Kelly had hired a small orchestra for the event. The owner of St. Malos was persuaded to close his restaurant for the evening and the menu choices epitomized the finest French cuisine. To prepare for this extravaganza, Colleen, Jeanne and "Kimbo" surveyed the formal wear being carried in their respective back packs and decided to initiate a shopping trip for the record books, through some of the Gold Coast's finest second-time-around clothing stores.

Kelly Small had inherited a small fortune but I think his life started out in a very unexceptional way, which might explain his down-to-earth attitude. His father, Sir Bruce Small, had made a lot of money starting up, developing, then selling the Malvern Star Bicycle Company. He then went into land development. Kelly was largely unaffected by this, having grown up before the wealth could have an effect on him. He spent part of the Second World War in the army, although he was probably too young to be posted overseas and see any combat. At war's end, he spent many years working with his father and eventually managed to keep the cash registers ringing after his father's death. During this time, I believe, Kelly missed the opportunity to create something which he could really call his own. This is why he bought Eracom. His real hero was Sir Hubert "Oppy" Opperman, the champion cyclist who had been sponsored by Malvern Star.

The Small empire never ceased to amaze me. It was nothing to receive a telephone call from, say, the Argentine embassy, in Canberra, asking about some repairs to the building where the embassy was housed, and then to discover that the building was owned by the Smalls. When I required an office in Melbourne, it was a matter of finding out what space might be available in one of the many Small-owned buildings in that city. We ended up getting a ground-floor office in the tallest building, along the waterfront, in the suburb of St. Kilda.

Christa Small's cousin, Ulrike, worked for Bruce Small Enterprises and we became friends with "Ully" and her husband, Hans. One time, we spent a weekend at the Small country property near Stanthorpe, in Queensland's apple orchard country. The property itself was huge and it was managed by farm workers who lived in four houses clustered around a country mansion, almost like a European country village. Prior to our weekend visit, the staff cleaned the house, made the beds and ensured that a fire was lit and essential foodstuffs were available. Hans was into kangaroo shooting and had a bull terrier which shared his enthusiasm, in stark contrast to our red setter puppy, Rusty, brought along on the weekend. The property had several vehicles available but we chose an ex-German army, 4-wheel-drive vehicle for a safari through the bush. Hans got his kangaroo, which was later barbecued, minus the parts the bull terrier had chomped on, while Rusty squeezed between my legs to hide from the carnage.

Christa Small was Kelly's second wife; she was ten, or so, years younger than he was but her influence on Kelly was strong. She was introduced to Kelly by her mother, who had worked for Kelly in Melbourne, before he moved to the Gold Coast. One had the impression that, here was a mother setting up her daughter with a wealthy man, for the Small family would have been one of the richest in Australia at the time. Christa was always impeccably groomed in a rather conservative style, appearing very much as I imagined a wealthy German lady would look. I found her quite cold and extremely difficult to decipher. Christa's hold over Kelly would later prove to be my downfall at Eracom and result in legal problems for the Small family.

For all their wealth, however, the Small family also had it's problems and tragedies. Kelly had his ambitions and a desire for his own claim to fame to match that of his father. Using Eracom as the spark to start a "Silicon Paradise" was a major part of that. He had other problems though and his son, Roger, was a lost soul. Roger was in his early 30s when I came to the Gold Coast; he had no job nor, indeed, any need for one. He lived in the fast lane and was known for being a heavy drinker. I liked him and we had a few good times together but he quickly got past the point of the happy drunk and became quite unintelligible. Kelly would try to interest Roger in anything which might prod him to get off the booze. One project, which Kelly's estate manager was persuaded to arrange, was to truck in several hundred beef cattle from Stanthorpe and have Roger manage a feed lot and some grazing pasture on land that was later to become the suburb of Benowa Waters. The project seemed to have started off well but it wasn't long before our office received an urgent call from the police telling us that a herd of cattle was wandering down Benowa Road and into the gardens around this new subdivision. While all of this was going on, Roger, it turned out, was out of action in the Benowa Tavern. That incident was my one and only experience at cattle mustering.

But the incident underscored the fact that Roger was seriously affected by his heavy drinking and his health rapidly deteriorated as time went by. I remember visiting him for the last time when he was being cared for by a relatively new girlfriend, while his father and Christa were overseas on a trip. In fact, he died while they were still away which only added to the pathos of the situation. How someone with so much going for him in life could descend to such dismal depths and die in his mid-30s is hard to believe and even harder to watch.

Kelly's only other child was his daughter, Anne, who was a doctor at the Melbourne Children's Hospital. She showed no interest in the family business. She was perhaps more involved in the social life in Melbourne which, in the early eighties, would not have been compatible with Queensland mores.

Throughout my life, there have been huge changes in attitudes to social issues—women's liberation, gay rights, acceptance of cultural differences, non-white immigration, non-marital (de facto) partnerships, and so forth—but, when it came to social change, Queensland seemed to lag behind other states and Western nations, by a decade or more. Also, the pace of life in Queensland was slower and this had to be taken into account when waiting for decisions to be made by businesses or other organisations. This difference was even more pronounced in

Brisbane and other parts of Queensland, because the Gold Coast was quite cosmopolitan and the majority of residents seem to have originated from elsewhere.

In 1982, we hosted a New Year's Eve party at our house and, since Anne was in town, we invited her and her three female friends from Melbourne. They were great fun but their Victorian lack of sexuality was quite obvious. Colleen displayed her mischievous streak when she challenged a couple of invited macho Queensland blokes, betting that they couldn't get anywhere with two of Anne's good looking friends. We delighted in witnessing the futility of the men's outpouring of charm as they tried to woo those females. They got nowhere with the girls. To soothe their wounded egos, the macho guys turned to arm wrestling as a party diversion with some of the guests.

Kelly was very much a social animal and he would never refuse a chance to party with us. One time, while his wife Christa was away in Germany, visiting her family, we invited Kelly to our house for dinner and a few drinks. He brought along his two Weimaraner hunting dogs and, as always, made for great company. That evening, Kelly discovered that I had asked Colleen to marry me and he took it upon himself to help persuade her to say, "Yes." It turned into a long, drinking evening and, by the end of the night, Colleen, Jeanne and I had gone to bed, leaving Kelly to find his way home. For years, thereafter, he would claim that the dogs had driven him home.

Having made himself partly responsible for Colleen's decision, Kelly undertook to furnish whatever support was needed for the forthcoming marriage. Since Colleen's parents could not make the trip to Australia, he offered to act as surrogate father and walk Colleen down the church aisle. This meant that she would be making all her bridal preparations at the Small's mansion and borrowing some of the Small family's jewellery. Colleen couldn't drive herself to the church, so Kelly got his friend, Max

Christmas, to drive her in his yellow Rolls Royce. The reception was held at a Kelly Small favourite, the St. Malos restaurant.

For Colleen and me, the wedding reception at St. Malos was part of a day that remains one of our greatest. Yet, it was also a most unusual wedding. We tied the knot at the Uniting Church, on Clifford Street, in Surfers Paradise—a little, old, wooden structure which no longer exists. It stood on the site that now forms the base for what became the world's tallest residential high-rise. Garth Filmer, a charming country reverend with five children, married us with the stern admonition that marriage was not something you got off the back of a cereal box. His sermon was so very Australian; and he asked God to "Bless this beaut couple."

Twenty-five years later, it is difficult to imagine the scene, that day, when you stand at a corner in today's Surfers Paradise. Garth joined us at the reception, with our mishmash of friends and workmates, and the photographs show him laughing with the Maid of Honour, while standing under a St. Malos picture of a high-kicking cancan dancer. Kelly was a party lover of the older generation, and was not amused when a party lover of the younger generation offered him a joint. The culprit, a surfboard manufacturer by the name of "Squeak," was quickly ushered out of the restaurant.

If I recall correctly, this was our last visit to St. Malos with Kelly because, some time later, Christa informed us that Kelly had been having an affair with the St. Malos waitress while Christa was away in Germany. As a result, she and Kelly would no longer patronise St. Malos. Now, I found her story of an affair pretty hard to believe, the more likely explanation being that Christa had convinced herself of something that had never happened. This was not an isolated incident of its kind. Former friends and associates would suddenly disappear from the Small's social network. I recall the time when a former army colleague of Kelly's, who was a director at Eracom and took part in my initial job interview, was no longer showing up with his wife in the company of the Small's. When I queried Christa on their whereabouts, she whispered that those people were not to be mentioned again. From that, I inferred that Christa had quarrelled with them over some real or imagined incident.

CHAPTER 14

RAISING THE ODDS

I NEVER STOP THINKING about business opportunities, even those that might not be very realistic. I had planned my move to Australia to take up the position with Eracom but the thought crossed my mind that there might be other opportunities for me in the, so called, Lucky Country. I knew that I would be catching up with Colleen and Jeanne in Australia and that they would be looking for work. What if I could find some product or service to introduce in Australia which would create an employment opening for both of them? That would almost triple my investment, in a single stroke.

One of my acquaintances in Toronto was the president of Remanco Corporation, a company making restaurant management systems. They were hugely successful throughout North America but Australia was a complete unknown to them. The president agreed to give me a window of opportunity, if I could exploit it. His company would train Colleen and Jeanne in the basic fundamentals of the system so that I could use them as sales representatives. He would provide us with an initial supply of promotional material and, if we found any prospects with a serious interest in buying a Remanco System, I was promised all the support I needed to close the deal.

This turned out very much like my earlier attempts to sell Micos in Australia. At that time, Australia ran restaurants in a manner very different to the practices common in North America.

Staff were paid realistic hourly wages—because tipping was not a common practice—and these wages would attract overtime rates for evenings and weekends. Most restaurants were small, family-owned businesses, so they had no need to hire staff at the higher rates of pay expected, and there were almost no large restaurant chains like those in North America. Restaurant owners would keep one set of books for themselves and another for the tax department, and they all expected to get ripped off by their employees. With such a vastly different business culture, there was a near-zero chance of getting some quick sales for Remanco. It pays to know your market thoroughly before trying to launch a new business.

There's another example of a business I investigated, only to find that market conditions in Australia made it unworkable. My friend, Bob Russell from Minitech days—you will remember colourful Bob, who had hired two, one-legged computer programmers for his company in Montreal and also got undressed in the Canadian Customs hall, at the Canada-U.S. border—had developed a business selling magazine subscriptions by mail order and targeting a number of markets, based on the mailing lists that he could buy. The business was a great success and still is, today. A particularly successful target market for Bob's company was the teaching profession, throughout the U.S. and Canada. In North America, the difference between the newsstand price and the price of a magazine obtained by subscription was quite large. In addition, there were large margins offered by magazine publishers to companies which managed subscriptions. In other words, this was a stellar money-making opportunity.

In Australia at that time, newsagents (shopkeepers who sell newspapers, magazines and stationery, and often lottery tickets) had exclusive distribution rights for magazines and papers, thus publishers were unable to offer their products through any other channels. This restriction has been eased in recent years but it still does not offer an opportunity to build a magazine subscription business. It is one example of the many restrictive trade practices in Australia, compared to North America, which result in consumers paying more for products. For an entrepreneur contemplating the migration of a business from another part of the world, it is vital to check the differing regulations covering the provision of a product or service. I learned this lesson the hard way.

With Colleen as my wife, it was time to start another business and one which she could run. Word processing was the new buzzword in office automation, although most Gold Coast offices were still strictly wedded to their IBM Selectric electric typewriters. A former girlfriend of Kelly's son, Roger, was running a secretarial service in Southport but she had no desire to upgrade from her "golf ball" element IBM typewriter and offer a word processing service. She was keen however to share offices with Colleen and pass on to her any of that new-fangled business. It was a simple matter to set up Colleen with an Eracom ERA-50 computer and a copy of Wordstar word processing software, and she was in business. This was still before Microsoft had released their word processing software, which was originally written by them for Apple. The new company was called WordPro and pretty soon, Gold Coasters would recognise the bright yellow Mini Moke buzzing around town with WordPro painted on its sides. The only problem with delivering computer printouts in a Mini Moke—basically, a small Jeep-like vehicle, open on all sides, with a canvas sunroof—is that a couple of sheets of continuous-form paper can blow out of the car, and take with them a confetti-like trail of computer output swirling down the road. And that's exactly what happened, one day, to a batch of printout belonging to our accountant and containing confidential information on clients from all over the Gold Coast. This slight glitch did not stop WordPro from becoming successful and moving into new premises, hiring new staff and taking on new responsibilities.

Meanwhile, I persisted with growing Eracom, or at least that part of it which I could control. Dr. Bill Caelli carried on running his own research department, along with his physicist colleagues. Kelly kept reminding me that Eracom was costing him a million dollars each year and wondering when it would make a profit. But, if I even hinted that, perhaps the research department should be trimmed, Kelly would terminate the conversation, then and there. I decided it might be better to find a way out for Kelly and I started making discreet enquiries about finding a potential buyer, at least for the business side of the company. That turned out to be relatively easy and I arranged for the business development officer of a Sydney-based public company to visit the Gold Coast for a preliminary meeting with Kelly. A date was confirmed on both sides and the Sydney executive flew in, for our meeting in Kelly's office. To my amazement, Kelly did not turn up for the meeting and, after several embarrassing hours, I returned the visitor to Coolangatta Airport for his flight back to Sydney.

It soon became clear that I was dealing with a very emotional subject—and one that involved not only Kelly. Christa was drawn in too. I later realised that she had completely misconstrued my motives and figured that I was trying to take over Kelly's company. How I could take over a company without having a dollar to invest for such an acquisition was not even considered. She acted purely out of emotion. Things quickly went downhill and my position at Eracom was terminated.

I had joined the St. Malos waitress and the former director of Eracom as banished people who were not to be talked about. I had no further contact with Christa, and I was thankful for that, but I did occasionally run into Kelly and certainly held no hard feelings towards him. Sadly, he died in 2003, at the age of 80, a very lonely soul. By that time, Christa had already left him for another man. I remember the last time I saw him; it was at the Benowa shopping centre, in the company of a paid carer. He was a very crestfallen sight. The family story is an absolute tragedy, in stark contrast to the Small's earlier achievements.

We attended Kelly's funeral, at which there were two groups of mourners, one led by Christa and the other by Kelly's daughter, Anne. There was no communication between the two. I did hear later that Anne had taken a successful legal action against Christa concerning Anne's rightful inheritance of the Kelly estate.

So, I was once more thrown to the wolves. I still had children to support in Canada, plus an obligation to visit them or have them visit me. Here I was, unemployed and—aside from our equity in our mortgaged house—broke.

To fill this sudden gap in my life, I immediately hired myself as business development manager at WordPro and decided to ramp up that business. Colleen had been developing things in a number of directions, one being the retailing of computer supplies including computer paper, floppy diskettes and printer ribbons. Her activities were aimed at supporting herself with supplies but occasionally obtaining these items for her clients. There was no supplier of such items on the Gold Coast so everything had to be sourced from Brisbane. My first action was to target a number of suppliers including Computer Resources, in Sydney, a ribbon company in Brisbane and a computer furniture company in Melbourne. We were in the right place at the right time so it was fairly easy to become the Gold Coast distributor for these firms.

We bought a new van, had it signed with WordPro and I settled in to become a salesman and delivery driver. It was the start of a good business but as with all businesses it does take time to get established and generate a decent income for the two of us.

Thus, I was constantly on the lookout for new opportunities and would sometimes purchase a bundle of items which I thought might be popular with customers on the Gold Coast. Colleen was taken aback, one day, when a stack of large cartons arrived at our small office and I announced that we were now selling brochure holders. Today, these injection-moulded brochure and display holders are ubiquitous but this was the first time I had seen them. I figured they would be very useful on the counters of retail businesses, especially outlets in the tourism sector. They were not all one size so I had to buy a carton of each holder to have the full range. We started advertising around Queensland, where we were the only company selling them, and the orders poured in. I recall the thrill of receiving the first order from Cairns, an early mecca of overseas tourism in Queensland.

The company we represented was Taymar Brochure Holders and they are still around today. One day, in 1985, Taymar's owner drove the 1,000-kilometre trip north from Sydney to see us. That was the first time I saw a mobile phone (the Aussie word for cell phone). He had phoned us for directions and, when I asked him where he was, the exchange went something like this:

"I'm in my car at Tweed Heads," he replied.

"What?" I blurted, "You've got a phone in your car?"

Anyone under the age of 40 would find it hard to understand my incredulity. I gave him directions and later he pulled up in front of our office with a mobile phone in his hand—part of it, anyway; the rest was in a box on the car floor.

One of the joys of starting and running your own business is meeting and working with other entrepreneurs who inspire and entertain you. I forget the name of "Mr. Taymar" but he was one of them.

Thanks to another entrepreneur, we expanded our WordPro company into the field of software sales. Clive Rainbow had developed one of the first 4GL database systems and was marketing it from his Sydney base as a package to computerise sales and marketing. The application was called SAMM and, as far as I know, was one of the first CRM systems. Clive had teamed up with Bob Hannon and Geoff Fuller, two Brisbane based sales trainers, and had devised a method of selling complete hardware and software packages based around SAMM. The instructions built into the software were followed in order to find leads for SAMM, then progress through to prospects and ultimately to customers. WordPro took on the distribution of the product in the Gold Coast-Tweed Heads area.

Around this time, Colleen's friend, Jeanne, returned to live in Australia and wondered whether we could help her obtain a visa. Not one to turn down a challenge, I hired Jeanne as a key employee, responsible for the sales of, and client training on, SAMM. Visa regulations allowed us to recruit someone from overseas if we had already advertised the job in Australia and had not found a suitable applicant. Jeanne was a qualified teacher and had experience with computers, so both attributes were included in the job description. We advertised the job in a rather obscure newspaper during the Christmas season and didn't receive any applications. We had followed the legal requirements and Jeanne joined the SAMM team on the Gold Coast.

After some product training and team-building meetings with the Sydney people, at an Armidale golf course, we were primed to close the first sales. We followed the instructions in every detail and I think we sold about a dozen systems in the Gold Coast area. This was a significant milestone, considering that a powerful personal computer connected to a decent printer and the SAMM software would cost $20,000, in today's money. Our clients were car dealers, real estate agents, holiday accommodation renters and time-share sales agents. Still, generating enough sales to keep four people employed was somewhat of a struggle. Also, I needed to support three children in Canada. When Jeanne decided to return to Canada, and sales were still at a trickle, I knew I had to get another job and leave Colleen and her assistant to run WordPro without us. When I spotted a job advertisement for a general manager at a Brisbane computer-assisted design company, it sparked the next chapter in my entrepreneurial career.

CHAPTER 15

❋

ACROSS AUSTRALIA'S OUTBACK

PALETTE SYSTEMS WAS FORMED by a University of Queensland lecturer, Dr. Michael McLean. He had established a leadership position in computer-assisted design (CAD) before expanding his business to the United States and leaving his assistant to run the Australian operation. Now, he wanted his assistant to join him in America, so he was looking for a general manager to oversee the Australian market. I was determined to be that man. As I had done when I applied for the position at Eracom, I could see myself in the job, so I covered all bases to be selected for the position. There are times in your life when you can picture success at some task and you move heaven and earth in order to make it happen. It worked with Palette Systems.

As was the case with Eracom, I inherited some baggage with the new position. Eracom had its dishonest Los Angeles sales consultant who had milked the company, and Palette had a high-flying salesman in Sydney who was costing more than he was worth. One of my first tasks was to replace him and find someone who could do the job better for less money. Palette's technical support person in Sydney was a Canadian by the name of Don Dunbar and he was well respected by customers and employees. Rather than hunt for a new and untried employee, I offered the position to Don. For an information technology consultant, Don Dunbar had a very interesting background. He had been trained as a pilot in Canada and became an instructor on DC-8 passenger jets for an airline. How he ended up working for Palette, in Sydney, is still a mystery to me.

Having Don on the team had its advantages. We often chartered an aircraft to visit business prospects who were a great distance away. Don's ability to fly in all weathers overcame the bad-weather delays that most private pilots frequently dealt with. Having a pilot on staff meant that we could travel by private plane and still save money by not flying with a commercial airline.

In 1986, we exploited this to the limit when we had a trade show to attend in Perth, at the opposite end of the Australian continent—by air, 3,600 km away from Gold Coast—or, if you like, the distance from Los Angeles to Washington, D.C. I did the numbers and could show my boss in America, Michael McLean, that we were saving him money by chartering a twin-engined Piper Navajo to fly to Perth and back. We decided to take our wives along, including Don and Denise's small baby, expend three days off on the way there and another three days for the return. That way, we would experience some of the vastness of Australia.

We flew out from Gold Coast's airport, Coolangatta, to a sheep station west of Charleville, in Queensland's outback, for which we had map coordinates and a description of intersecting runways, only one of which was in use. Don's navigation skills got us pretty close to the station and then we had to scan the ground carefully to spot the drought-parched airstrip, which was next to an abandoned farmhouse. There was no telling which runway was the operational one, so we took our chances and ended up touching down on the strip that hadn't been used for years, dodging small bushes before taxiing to a stop.

We stepped out of the plane into a cloud of flies and wandered through the deserted farmhouse. It was several years since anyone had lived there but it could have been just yesterday. The house was furnished and stocked with cooking utensils, dishes, cutlery and even a few old cans of food. It was an eerie spectacle, made more uncanny by the silence of the countryside. We were miles from the nearest road.

An hour later, we glimpsed a dust cloud in the distance and pretty soon a dilapidated Chrysler station wagon drove up and stopped. Out jumped a rugged looking farmer in a weather-beaten hat and his first words were, "Wanna stubby?" A stubby is the Aussie word for a bottle of beer. The Chrysler still had American-style air conditioning and an Aussie Esky (that's short for food and beverage cooler) in the back of the car. It had been stocked with the coldest "XXXX" brand of Queensland beer stubbies you could hope to find, anywhere. Our sudden host was an interesting and obviously hospitable bloke. He took us on the half-hour drive, through paddocks of sheep, kangaroos and emus, to his station. We would be staying in the sheep shearer's quarters which turned out to be quite modern. Next day, he arranged for us to visit a neighbour where sheep shearing was taking place.

He had three children, two of them at boarding school, and the boy still at home was so kindled by having visitors he was virtually bouncing off the walls. He was learning via the School of the Air, a two-way, short-wave radio classroom for children in remote locations of Australia, and we were able to watch him tune in, to listen to his teacher in class. "Have you done your homework?" she asked; "Over. . ." The father and mother were extremely well informed about world affairs. It surprised us how much our hosts knew about Canadian politics. They were far better informed than anyone we had met in the cities. Their source of information was Radio Australia; that was the only broadcast they received.

After Charleville, we set our bearings for Ayers Rock, in Northern Territory, and took the best part of a day to cover the distance. On the way, we stopped for lunch at Birdsville, a great place for a break because you can taxi the aircraft right up to the Birdsville Pub. Our pilot, of course, would have to wait for a stubby until we got to Ayers Rock. Having learned to fly in Canada, I felt relieved that the piloting responsibility was not all mine now.

We spotted Ayers Rock—known officially by its aboriginal name of Uluru—from 50 miles away and, as we flew by, Don buzzed The Rock at low altitude. That's something he probably would not try today because this iconic outcrop—jutting out starkly in the middle of a vast and empty plain—is sacred to Australia's aborigines and the Australian nation has become increasingly sensitive to indigenous rights and traditions. Upon landing and settling in at the Yulara Resort, we waited until sunset to watch Ayers Rock changing colour as the light from the dipping sun bathed this sandstone monolith—the world's largest monolith—at a progressively lower angle, until twilight gave it a final, spectacular glow. Next day, we climbed to the top of Uluru and I wonder how much longer this will be possible, given the recent recognition of aboriginal spiritual feelings.

After another night at Uluru, we flew past The Olgas (Kata Tjuta, to aborigines) and across the Great Victoria Desert, on our way to Kalgoorlie. What a massive country this is—and most of it is desert; Australia is 59 times the size of my native England! Kalgoorlie is an oasis in the middle of it all, only because of the discovery of gold, back in the nineteenth century. Today, we have the luxury of dropping in on places that took the early pioneers weeks to travel to. I have a great deal of respect for them; talk about toughing it out: those pioneers were the toughest of all.

We spent a day in Kalgoorlie and went down an old underground mine. Years later, in 2011, I returned to Kalgoorlie on a different business venture and the mine that I had visited was gone, swallowed up by a 1-kilometre-deep superpit. This country has undergone so many changes in the short time I have been here.

The final leg of our flight was a day-long hop to Perth. Now, it was time for work but, no matter what we achieved at the computer show, it would pale into insignificance against our journey across the continent.

At the close of the trade show, we looked forward to our return flight. We had planned to visit the south-western corner of Western Australia but bad weather changed that and we headed east, toward the Nullarbor Plain. We landed for fuel at a place called Forrest and realised that we could not fly further that day because our next planned stop was Coober Pedy, in South Australia, and their airport did not have runway lights. I asked the guy refuelling our aircraft if there was a motel in town and he broke up laughing. There was not even a road. This place was just a railway maintenance depot and a weather station. In fact, Forrest lies on the world's longest straight stretch of railway, a 478-kilometre steel straightedge cutting across the treeless Nullarbor Plain, a vast plateau that remains a largely unpopulated and inhospitable region.

He suggested that the weather station might have a spare house. We found a place to stay for the night and, at some point in the future, the meteorological office in Canberra would send us an invoice for this. The wife of the weather station operator apologised that she could not entertain us because they were planning a rare trip to visit their neighbours, the railway people. She gave us a frozen chicken and some vegetables, plus a video of the previous week's TV programs and wished us a pleasant evening. It turns out that the "Tea and Sugar" train comes through, once a week, and that's how they purchase their groceries and obtain videos of the previous week's television programs. Our weather hostess was pretty sure she was pregnant, and she was waiting for confirmation of this during the next monthly visit, by air, of the Royal Flying Doctor Service.

Forrest is a magic spot on the planet. After the power-supply generator was turned off, the place became totally silent and the night sky put on a spectacular show of a million stars. It was something I had never seen before; nor have I seen it since.

The weather people were fascinated to hear we were from Canada because, during Christmas, they had exchanged radio greetings with the remotest weather station in Canada. On Christmas Day, the temperature in Forrest was a sizzling 47°C (117°F) while, at this weather station in the Yukon, the thermometer had plunged to -47°C (-53°F). When the Forrest couple went to check on their chooks (chickens) that day, they found all of them had died from the heat.

We waved farewell, next day, to our new meteorological friends and headed for Coober Pedy. This town is famous for opal mining and it is such an inhospitable place that most people choose to live underground, in caves which were formerly mining tunnels. The rock is a soft, white, dry material—almost like clay without moisture—so when it is cut it actually makes for nice internal walls, like plaster. We stayed overnight at the Underground Motel and the rooms were attractive and comfortable, with tiled floors and varnished walls. The single biggest national group in Coober Pedy is of Greek origin. We met several people who had never been anywhere else in Australia, except for the drive from Adelaide Airport to Coober Pedy. It is a bizarre place, indeed, but one where fortunes can be made. Opal mining is just about the only mining enterprise which has not been taken over by big business and the place is full of old prospectors. They all tell stories about other miners who had struck it rich and they cling to the same dream for themselves. It is rather like my mother's dream: she often told what she would do when she won the football pools.

The following day, after a brief refuelling stop in Broken Hill, at the western edge of New South Wales, we arrived in Sydney where Don Dunbar lives. Colleen and I took a commercial airline flight to return to the Gold Coast. I cannot think of it otherwise: this had been the trip of a lifetime.

Palette Systems had a very loyal user base across Australia and one of the things the company did very well was run an annual user conference. This became one of our best marketing efforts each year and was attended by most of our customers, many of whom were large engineering firms, local and State government departments, mining companies and heavy manufacturers and shipbuilders. The conference program was fairly technical and allowed Palette to encourage users to employ all the new features of the software. It became a forum for users to discuss a wish list of new capabilities they would like to see in an upgraded system. The highlight was the conference dinner, at which we would hire a well known comedian for entertainment. Not all companies have the need for a business conference but for those that do, it can be an extremely good vehicle for communicating with your customers. For Palette Systems, it was an annual event that the company and the customers looked forward to.

At Palette Systems, I had some interesting experiences in dealing with governments, especially one like Queensland's National Party, headed by Sir Joh Bjelke-Petersen. At the time, our software was widely used for mapping and as an early version of a Land Information System. As a result, I met with the head of the Queensland Department of Lands and, after explaining to him all about Palette Systems and what we could do for the government, I asked what we could do to win some business with his department. The response was, "Well, you can start by taking me to lunch!" The intent was not to grab a sandwich on that day but to set a date and choose a nice restaurant to wine and dine him the following week. I found this incident amusing but the next experience was a little more serious.

Queensland Rail were interested in computerising their maps and plans of the main railway line from Brisbane to Cairns. Some of the plans dated back many years and most were annotated in Imperial measurements, including yards and furlongs. Mike McLean came up with a system design which would automate the creation of a database from which new maps could be produced with metric measurements. All of the old maps identified the position of objects by their distance from Brisbane and the offset of the object from the track. Mike determined that a table could be produced into which these distances and offsets would be entered. He would then write a computer program to interpret this database and redraw the maps in the Palette System.

The design was used as the basis for a tender for the supply of a complete new system for Queensland Rail which would represent a contract for over a million dollars. We continued to have contact with the proposed users since we had been the originators of the design of the system and the buying signals we received from this group were strong. So good were our contacts that, when the evaluation committee made their recommendation, we received a call to confirm that Palette Systems had been selected and the recommendation had gone to the government Cabinet. The tender process included a public opening of the tenders and a declaration of the total amount quoted so we were already aware that we were the lowest bidder. We were also the only Queensland company bidding. We must have been in the box seat. Imagine our surprise, then, after Cabinet came back with their decision that the contract would go to Prime Computer, an American company. I later found out that Prime had made a large donation to the National Party at the last moment before this Cabinet decision.

Mike McLean was in America but he asked me to issue a public statement that we were challenging the decision of the government and would identify our reasons why. By then, we knew that we were the low bidder, we were the only bidder to meet all the technical requirements of the tender, and we were the only local company bidding. The Queensland Government at that time was embroiled in a number of matters relating to government corruption, so the media were interested in hearing our story. I was interviewed for the evening news and several current affairs programs and the newspapers gave us full coverage of the situation. It was all to no avail however. In Queensland, in the 1980s, a political donation beats supplier competence, anytime, and we had to move on and put the matter behind us. The experience left me somewhat cynical of government contracts and I have experienced a number of disappointments of a similar, but not quite so brazen, nature since then. I have come to the conclusion that I am not very good at dealing with governments.

Palette Systems continued to prosper but Mike McLean began to focus on other opportunities in America and we realised that our product was no longer at the cutting edge. Although it was not my company, I recognised that it was time for an exit strategy. The company still had many market advantages and there were other companies which complemented what we did and which, if the two were combined, would increase the value of Palette. One such company was Computeracc, which sold solutions to local governments. Palette had good graphics software for the mapping of local government operations so, together, the combined value was stronger. By coincidence, I had been working with another company that was wooing Computeracc and that was Computer Power. Also by coincidence, I had recently been on a trade mission to Japan with the CEO of Computer Power and so it was fortunate that I could size up an opportunity for Mike McLean to sell his Australian operation. The result was a move by Computeracc to buy Palette and at the same time a move by Computer Power to buy Computeracc. I ended up working for new bosses based in Melbourne.

Mike McLean rewarded me with a nice bonus but I was not happy working as part of the new larger company and I started thinking about new ventures. As an aside, the bonus went into the stock market via my superannuation fund, just days before the 1987 stock market crash. Sometimes, you can't win, no matter what you do!

During my three-year tenure at Palette, things had not remained the same at WordPro. When I moved on, and Colleen was left to run the business with one employee, she started hankering for a change, so we decided to put the company up for sale. I prepared a document which showed the company in it's best light and contacted the business broker at Max Christmas Real Estate. He indicated that we would have no problem selling the business and he was right. Within a couple of weeks, he had found a buyer who was willing to give us the price we were looking for. We should have been ecstatic but, for some reason, we had apprehensions about whether our "baby" could be properly managed by the prospective buyer. The buyer was Fred Spiegel, a former concrete truck driver with thick glasses, who wore very thick-soled running shoes and a sloppy sweatshirt. A very nice guy but could he be trusted with WordPro? I know the feeling was silly and ultimately we had to let go and sign the business over to Fred. We couldn't see how a guy in running shoes and a sweatshirt could run a business, but we were wrong. Fred went on to own WordPro for several years and, as far as we know, he never had a single problem doing so. It shows how emotions can interfere with business in the strangest ways.

Colleen also moved into the corporate world for a short term, working as a convention organiser at Conrad Jupiter's Casino, at Broadbeach. She struggled with the move from self-employed independent business woman to become part of the 2,000-employee Conrad Jupiter's team. She also discovered that the world of international hotel management is very demanding, in terms of the hours required on site, especially when a conference was taking place. She decided it was not for her.

CHAPTER 16

*

THE BIRTH OF ORION

With the possibility that Colleen might again become available for a new business opportunity, it was fortunate that an old colleague from Canada had approached me about a business we could become involved with. One of my old friends, Ernest Priess had been involved as a consultant in starting the first lottery in Canada, the Olympic Lottery of 1967, which had evolved into the government-owned Lotto Canada. Ernie was just too much of an independent free wheeler to be employed by a government lottery but he didn't stop thinking about how to promote them. His had become the first company to buy lottery tickets in Canada and sell them by mail order to Americans. Lacking a lottery of any kind in the USA, Americans were willing to pay double the price for the opportunity to play the Canadian lottery. Ernie's company, Winshare, offered a regular subscription service to play the same numbers every week and in return they would receive a newsletter of results and stories about winners, all conveniently paid for by credit card over the phone. At that time Winshare was turning over several million dollars every month.

Ernie's approach to me was for us to source Australian lottery entries which Winshare could also offer to it's clients and at the same time we could build our own database of customers which we would share with Winshare. The key to the whole business was to set up the appropriate systems and take advantage of advertising methods which Ernie had pioneered with Winshare. We flew to Canada to meet with the Winshare people and learn what their requirements were for the Canadian company and to discover how we could develop our own operation back in Australia. Ernie Priess came up with the clever name of Orion International, for our Australian company, because the constellation Orion is visible in both northern and southern hemispheres. The name Orion refers to the hunter, in Greek mythology, and I liked the idea. I used the name "Orion" for three further companies we established, later on.

The company started operating on the dining table of our home in Benowa Waters and Colleen hired two girls to help her send out mass mailings to the USA, enter the orders into the computers, fill out the lottery entries and go down to the newsagent with bundles of cash. It was a very successful business and, considering the volume of transactions, it worked like a charm. We soon outgrew our dining room and we decided to invest in an office unit in Karp Court, Bundall. The company grew and we took advantage of our business trips back to Canada to spend time with my kids. It was on one of these trips that I was able to introduce my son, Richard, to Ernie resulting in Richard joining Winshare as a management trainee. Some months later, Richard and Ernie organised a plan for Richard to migrate to Australia in a transfer to Orion International.

The business was totally legal but we were buying from a government-operated lottery in Queensland and selling to places like California and Florida, before those states had started their own government lotteries. As a consequence, we were viewed as operating through loopholes and the bureaucrats were constantly trying to shut us down. Their bullying tactics ran as far as sending us a subpoena from the Florida Court to appear under some charge, in Miami. Ernie had been there before and told us to ignore it, but it did give us a few sleepless nights.

We worked with the authorities, however, and met with the head of the Queensland government lottery to explore the potential of gaining an officially approved government licence to handle international sales. The meeting was short and unproductive, with the lottery head speaking to us as if we were the enemy. Later, I would learn that our competitor was to follow the same process but he was to do so with a much more effective strategy. The competitor was Terry Morris, another Gold Coast entrepreneur, who I had met previously through the Rotary Club. Terry had retained a lawyer to act for him in convincing a State or Territory Government to provide some form of international licence. The lawyer was Paul Everingham, former Chief Minister of the Northern Territory, and readers may remember that it was Paul Everingham who represented us, in the court action I described at the start of this book. In this case, Paul was successful for Terry and it was a good lesson of always using the very best expertise when it is available. Terry's investment in Paul's services would be repaid more than a hundredfold.

Ernie visited Australia on one occasion, along with his girlfriend of the time, who was the daughter of the Prime Minister of St. Kitts in the Caribbean. It was interesting to meet someone who had been a guest to dinner with Queen Elisabeth II on the Royal Yacht Britannia. Ernie was operating several businesses in the Caribbean, including lotteries, a casino, an online florist and a noni-juice company. He tried to interest me in migrating some of these ideas to Australia but my conservative side kicked in and I kept my mind on Orion. During this visit I did arrange for a meeting with Terry Morris at which time Ernie raised the issue of his designs being used in Terry's promotions. We enjoyed a very civilised lunch at the Sheraton Mirage at which Ernie accused Terry of stealing his ideas and yet he did it in such a way that nobody was upset and a satisfactory commercial deal was reached. That was one very cool negotiation.

All this time, I was still working for Palette Systems which had now become a division of Computer Power and I was itching to get out on my own, again. Once more, I reached inside my networking toolkit and came up with a Vancouver company, by the name of Epic Data. I had dealt with them for bar-code equipment when I lived in Canada and they had progressed to become a leader in the field of shop-floor data collection systems. As far as I could tell, there was no competitor in Australia. I approached Epic in Canada and they confirmed that they had no business in Australia so anything I could do would be a positive move. Another Canadian holiday, with a visit to Epic Data in Vancouver, and another business was born. This was to be the second incarnation of the Orion name in the form of Orion Systems Pty Ltd. Why the focus on Canadian businesses? This was largely because I was looking for reasons to go back and visit my kids as often as possible, plus the fact that Canada was where my business roots were. This was 1988, and by then, my daughter, Alex, had left school and was flying with Wardair, while Angela was graduating from high school. On that trip, Alex was working the Wardair flight from Vancouver to Toronto, so I booked a ticket on her flight.

Upon returning to Australia, it was time to say goodbye to Palette and set up the new office for Orion Systems.

The launch of Orion Systems was timed to occur in September, 1988, at the Canadian pavilion of Expo 88 in Brisbane. Our sales rep from Epic Data, Kevin McHugh, came over to assist us at the launch and we persuaded the Canadian government to host receptions in Sydney and Melbourne to complete the promotion. I targeted the same kinds of companies that Epic already had as customers in the USA and these included Qantas, Hawker de Havilland, and Alcan, all of which later became customers. That was the most successful promotion I have ever done. We did the launch in September and by the following February both Qantas and Alcan signed up with us on the same day. As we waited for the orders to come from Qantas and Alcan, we played off one company against the other, encouraging them to stake their claim of being the first Australian customer. Now, I can't remember which one was first.

The Qantas system was a first of it's kind in Australia, automating data collection on the IBM mainframe computers at the Sydney maintenance base. The initial system tracked the issuing—and return—of tools from nine tool cribs around the Jet base, ensuring that tools were not left in sensitive areas, inside aircraft mainframes and engines.

The year 1988 was an exciting time in Australia for many reasons. Not only was Expo 88 being held in Brisbane but the Gold Coast was coming of age with international hotels and waterside developments happening all over the place. The previous year at the launch of the Sanctuary Cove gated community, Frank Sinatra and Whitney Houston had headlined the Ultimate Event. One of the exciting new developments was Australia's first private university, Bond University, named after it's founder Alan Bond. The concept was to develop an institution with a very close relationship to private industry along the lines of Stanford University in California and as a result they built a Research Park in order to attract technology based businesses that would hire future graduates. Orion Systems became the first commercial tenant in that new development. We were rapidly joined by a range of companies including bio-technology and software businesses, computer manufacturers like Digital and one of the first internet providers in Australia. Bond University was connected to an international data network called ARPANET, which would become the internet shortly after Bond was established. They were certainly in the forefront of IT development at that time, one that was to affect us profoundly in the future.

In hindsight, we did well to sign up two large multinationals as our first customers considering the fact that we were a small start-up company with no track record. I was very conscious of the fact that first impressions really do matter and I was determined to impress the team of Qantas engineers which flew to the Gold Coast to see us. Being a tenant at the brand new Bond University gave me access to some imposing meeting facilities. The result was that the challenge of creating a good first impression was certainly very different from the day when I fronted up in a Volkswagen in Winnipeg, Manitoba, for that University of Manitoba meeting, back in the early days of Comma.

One of our big advantages was the fact that Epic Data had installed some very impressive systems in the maintenance operations of United Airlines, American Airlines, Lufthansa and others, and I was able to make a presentation which had the Qantas engineers associating those achievements with Orion Systems. The engineers were onside, but the IT consultant who was heading the project was not. When the meeting descended into an argument between the engineers (who would be the users of the system) and the consultant, with the engineers speaking for our proposal, I knew we had a good chance of winning. We were one of nine companies bidding for the project and we found out after winning the business that the consultant had placed us 9th on his list. I think the reason for this was that the consultant had a fixed, PC-based architecture in his mind, into which we did not fit. What we did have, which our competitors did not, was proven installations with other airlines around the world. In another industry, that may not have carried as much weight but airline staff are different. They travel a lot and they work closely with other airlines. We went on to prove ourselves because that system remained in use for almost ten years.

Meanwhile, Orion International continued to flourish and with the start up of Orion Systems we were able to share a particular employee. I had hired a Japanese computer programmer by the name of Matsushita—we called him Mat—and we decided to try promoting the Australian lottery to the Japanese with a few ads in magazines. Ernie created a theme for us, a survey which ostensibly would research a person's luck. Japanese, being quite superstitious, would be tempted to respond to our promotion and we would then show them how lucky they could be if they played the Australian lottery. Once a person decided to subscribe to our service, they could call a toll-free number in Japan which would put the caller through to our number in Australia. It turns out that Orion International was the first company in Australia to utilise this service.

Mat would normally be the only person who would answer that line, but we did develop a backup telephone operator when Mat was not available. That person was Colleen. She had taken a course in Japanese conversation and we hired a marketing consultant to help us create a script that she could use with our Japanese clients. Her telephone script was quite condensed in that she informed the caller that her Japanese was not good, and asking if she could restrict the call to a few questions. In this way, she would take an order from the client or a name and phone number, so that Mat could return the call, later. Amazingly, it worked. I will always remember the day Colleen first tried the method and the surprise all of us had as we listened to her going through the script and completing the order.

The Japanese business grew but not at the rate we had experienced in North America. In hindsight, the reasons were quite obvious, but at the time we felt a little disappointed by the results. What we hadn't taken into account was the fact that our North American business was a more mature market and we were riding on the successes of many others, including our partners at Winshare. In Japan, we were pioneering a new market. I have found that new businesses always take a lot longer to grow to a breakeven point than is originally projected. Today, after pioneering a number of businesses entering new markets,

I would say that initial projections of growth to breakeven point are often wrong by a factor of two or three.

It was perhaps a year after we started our Japanese business that Colleen expressed a desire to move on to something else. She was getting tired of the repetitive business that was sometimes the day-to-day operations of Orion International. She wanted a new challenge. I decided to approach Terry Morris to see if he would be interested in buying our operation. He jumped at it and he made what was probably a very good deal for him. I was busy with Orion Systems which deterred me from getting more involved with the lottery business. In hindsight I should have found another way to continue with Orion International but Colleen was ready to move on so I convinced myself that the sale to Terry Morris was a good deal for me. One positive aspect of the deal was to learn from one of Australia's most successful entrepreneurs. Terry already owned a mail order company, the Gold Coast's largest retail market centre, a motor racing company, and Queensland's largest winery, complete with restaurant winery tours and concerts featuring international bands.

Our disappointment with the results of our Japanese marketing was quite unfounded. I ran into Terry Morris a couple of years after selling the business to him and he confessed that our original promotion for Japan was absolutely brilliant. The credit for the idea goes to Ernie but we can rightfully take credit for the execution of the scheme. We just did not have the patience to see the whole thing through and the lesson from the experience is that persistence is one of the major contributors to success in business.

After Orion International, Colleen prepared for some time off and a planned visit from her parents, but with her experience and personality, time off was not going to be a reality. She was interviewed for a job while her parents were visiting and by the time they departed she was employed as Marketing Manager at Neumann Steel on the Gold Coast.

Orion Systems started well, with Qantas and Alcan, as our first clients but we rapidly began to be affected by the decline in the economy. The 1987 stock market crash had wiped out a lot of my bonus from selling Palette. Bond Corporation and their Japanese partner EIE Corporation both got into financial trouble and a number of our neighbours at the Research Park disappeared. Interest rates rose to over 20 per cent per annum and we were big borrowers for the systems which we were importing from Canada. Manufacturing cutbacks began to dry up budgets to purchase the products we were selling. All this was happening while I was running a start-up company and trying to reach the breakeven point, now much further in the future than projected.

I had to cut back on some costs, abandoning some planned software development and reluctantly having to make Richard, Mat and another programmer redundant. I had to get out more, myself, to find new business and yet maintain a costly support service for both hardware and software. One of the luxuries that I fought to maintain was having the business based on the Gold Coast. Most of our new business opportunities were in Sydney and Melbourne but I enjoyed the lifestyle on the Coast and I would give up the business before I would relocate. Luckily, air fares got lower, especially if one could book in advance and purchase tickets for which the travel included a weekend away. The intent was to give holiday makers cheap fares while still charging higher fares for business travellers. I always booked two sets of travel, one originating on the Gold Coast, and one originating in Sydney so that I could meet these conditions. Sometimes I had four sets of tickets going, at one time, including Sydney and Melbourne.

We rented an apartment, and later a house, in Hurstville which would serve as an office and support centre, and double as a place for me to stay when in Sydney. The transfer of people from the Gold Coast to Sydney meant that I very soon did not require the office at Bond University, so I negotiated a release from the lease and took up space at a serviced office in Bundall.

Meanwhile, Orion made steady progress with new customers. Over the next five years, we would add big organisations to our customer list: Transfield Shipbuilding, Hawker de Havilland, Pilkington Glass, Western Mining, Siemens Plessey, NSW State Rail Authority, Transfield Construction, EDI Walkers, ACL Gasket, and others. We established cooperative marketing relationships with software companies like Cincom and Mincom and with other hardware companies for specialised scanners and printers.

I joined the Automatic Data Capture Association, ADCA, and in the early 1990s I was elected as chairman of the organisation. This was a good way to keep abreast of what was going on in the industry and to gain introductions to new opportunities. An organisation of this kind is also the best way to keep abreast of, and have some say in, the creation of regulations which are becoming much more a reality in running a business. In the case of ADCA's members, regulatory restrictions came from two areas, the barcode standards used in retailing and the fact that we used radio frequencies to transmit data from hand-held terminals to a computer database. As is frequently the case, Australian governments seem to select regulations that differ from those used in America or Europe. Finding out how to work with regulators and regulations is a key part of running any business.

CHAPTER 17

ORION'S DOG COLLAR

THE NEXT TEN YEARS were probably the toughest years of my business life. The economy was bad and we had a government that had legislated high levels of pay and benefits to be paid to employees. For some years, I was the lowest paid member of our company. It was also a time when technological developments were racing ahead. Epic Data had been extremely successful in the US defence manufacturing industry and heavy aircraft maintenance but that meant they did not need to develop products for other industries and opportunities. We could see new products being launched around us while Epic Data continued to run with it's own cash cow. The result was that Epic's products were gradually becoming obsolete and they did not realise it until it was too late. They had to resort to buying the handheld terminals from competitors to use in their systems.

I had recognised this threat for some time and had tried to diversify away from Epic Data with other products and services. We developed our own time-and-attendance software which could gather employee data for payroll systems but this was only marginally successful. We also took on the distributorship of Identicard Systems, from the USA, one of the leaders in employee identification systems in America. I think we were a little ahead of our time with those systems: we often received the reaction from Australians that they were different and would never wear name tags around their necks, the way Americans did. Time has shown that prediction to be wrong. From organisations like Qantas Airlines, who had adopted employee ID cards, we found that they had selected a different standard to the one being offered by the market leaders in America. Orion Systems was quite successful with ID cards and the supply-items business continued well after Orion Systems had stopped selling Epic Data products.

Again, I dipped into my deepening network to find ways of bolstering the revenue of Orion Systems. Richard Lapointe, one of Minitech's original partners, had developed MainBoss, a PC-based software package for maintenance management. We sold a number of these packages in Australia but the price level and the margins were insufficient to contribute much to our operation. This was the kind of software package which would end up as an online purchase, once the Internet became more widely accepted.

I also re-connected with Bob Russell, former CEO of Minitech, who went on to create a number of enterprises. One of his firms had developed a system for ship chandlers, called Ship Stores. Ship chandlers, or providores as they are sometimes called, are companies that supply ships with all manner of goods when the vessel visits a port. The business of supplying ships can be quite complex, including invoicing arrangements in multiple currencies, and sometimes incorporating secret commissions for ships' masters or agents. Designing a computer system for such a service requires a creative systems analyst and Bob was certainly one of them.

Bob had identified a prospective customer in Australia's largest ship chandler and he asked me to work with him in supplying and supporting the required hardware and software. He came to Australia, closed the deal with the client, and immediately started working with one of my programmers on customising and implementing the system. The implementation part was not an easy task. Aside from the unconventional business practices of the client, many of the PCs in use were quite old and too slow to support the network required by Ship Stores. The company reluctantly invested in the hardware for the pilot system at head office, but branch-wide implementation of the system was being resisted. Developing such a system gave us an inside view of the company's finances and we realised that getting paid for what we had supplied would have to be our number one priority. We did in fact get paid but, shortly thereafter, the company called in the receivers and was ultimately taken over by someone else. This was indicative of Australia's national economy at the time.

In the meantime, I downsized yet again by moving from the serviced office in Bundall back to an office in my home. When the economy did at last recover and organisations were increasing their IT budgets, technology had moved on and the shop floor data-collection terminal was being replaced with a PC. PCs had become cheap enough that, even if a PC was not sufficiently rugged for a long life in a factory, it didn't matter because they were easily replaced. By 1995, Orion Systems was making more money from it's maintenance services than from the sales of new systems. Without new products from Epic Data or some other supplier, the business would go into a slow decline.

It was at about this time that I discovered a product which was to become the basis of my next business venture, and perhaps my life's greatest challenge. An American firm, the Invisible Fence Company, had developed an electronic dog collar which would be activated if a dog tried to escape from its owner's property. The company had become very successful with a network of distributors across America who would supply and install the system and train the customer's dog to the system. The inventor of the invisible fence had a 25-year patent which prevented competitors from copying his idea and that patent ran out in the early-1990s. A number of companies had been waiting for the patent to run out and in 1995 I was able to find three companies which had the technology to supply a similar system and all three were willing to help me sell their systems in Australia. I selected the product from a company trading under the name of Innotek. I found out that Innotek had been producing similar dog training products for a few years and they appeared to have the best technology of the three. The other products were designed for different behavioural problems with dogs, such as nuisance barking or to provide off leash aversion training to discourage dogs from chasing cars, livestock, or wildlife, or to reinforce commands. I formed a new company, Orion Pet Products, and arranged for this company to be the exclusive distributor for Innotek in Australia.

I ordered a selection of Innotek's products and had them shipped to our Hurstville office, where our computer technicians could be employed to assemble, test and provide after- sales service for these electronic collars. The first hurdle to overcome was to generate demand by educating the market about what we had to offer. Our initial attempts to interest retailers in selling the products fell on deaf ears because, naturally, no consumers would be asking for a product they hadn't heard of. We created demand with a direct- marketing campaign, supported by public relations and our campaigns used print media, letter-box drops, the Internet, radio and TV. Slowly we gained the support of more and more retailers until, today, we have over 800 outlets selling our products.

Our biggest challenge to building this business reared it's ugly head after I sent out a press release announcing the availability of these products in Australia. A reporter called to ask me how I was going to get around the fact that electronic dog collars were an illegal import. An illegal import? I had no idea of such a restriction and obviously neither had Australian Customs because they had allowed my first delivery to come through. That could have been the end of the business, right there, but I decided to treat it as just another one of those hard business challenges. I decided to investigate the nature of the banned item and found the description listed alongside rocket launchers and hand grenades. Someone had a really bad view of electronic dog collars. The legislation defined the illegal import as "a dog collar, with a device attached, which is designed to impart an electric shock to the dog's skin". If the device was not attached to the collar, then the items being imported no longer met the description of the illegal import.

So, our future imports were of components for electronic dog collars and when the pressure was later applied to search all of our shipments, we even resorted to having collars and components freighted in separate shipments. The source of this strange legislation came from the National President of the Royal Society for the Prevention of Cruelty to Animals, and the organisation itself. Over the coming years, we would find ourselves under frequent attack from the RSPCA—and the government agencies which they had influenced.

The customs importation ban was only the first of many laws which the RSPCA had persuaded Australian governments to impose. It turned out that electronic collars were illegal in South Australia, the Australian Capital Territory, and New South Wales. By the time I had discovered the legal situation in all Australian states and territories, we had already sold a hundred or more collars and the response from dog owners was amazing. The solution which we were providing was achieving instant results in a humane manner and owners were claiming that we were saving dogs' lives. In addition, I was now using the containment system myself, having acquired a Dalmatian puppy, named Sparky. The name was chosen because, in North America, Sparky is the name of the Dalmatian mascots often used by city fire departments. In Australia, people thought we had chosen the name as some kind of sick joke because we sold electronic dog collars that could deliver electric sparks.

As far as the law was concerned, it was obvious to me that the RSPCA had responded in an emotional way at the thought of an electric shock being applied to an animal. They had no experience of what level of shock was applied and the beneficial results that could be achieved for dogs and dog owners. I decided to lobby anyone, who would listen, to change their point of view and ultimately change these misguided laws.

Our next attack from the RSPCA was in New South Wales, where we had assembled the products. The local inspector, Steven Coleman, now Chief Executive Officer of the RSPCA in New South Wales, called up our local office and arranged to see some of our products. He impersonated a dog owner interested in purchasing a collar for his dog. Our employee, Gaby, informed Coleman that he should contact our sales office in Queensland but Coleman must have been persuasive, because he was allowed to drop in to see the products. The following week, Coleman returned with his fellow officers and a video camera to charge our employee and to tape a sensational TV production for the nightly news. It turns out that what we were doing was not illegal because we were not using the collars on dogs in NSW. The truth did not matter, however, as is so often the case with the RSPCA's stories. The more important issue was to get publicity for the RSPCA to increase people's charitable donations and to build the organisation.

We had to successfully defend ourselves in this case, in order to avoid a situation which our opponents could use against us, forever. Almost more important than that, however, was the need for me to get our rattled employee, Gaby, off these charges because of the pressure he was feeling from the situation. The raid by four uniformed officers of the RSPCA had really distressed Gaby and he was talking about leaving the country to return to his native Lebanon. He was starting to think that Australia was more of a police state than his native land and he could not believe that this was all about dogs. Anyway, I assured him that we would do everything in our power to get him off and he should not worry.

We managed to find a very good barrister, a former attorney to the RSPCA, who was more than willing to act for us. The case was heard by a magistrate in the Kogorah Court and upon hearing of the circumstances of the case, the magistrate ordered the case to be dismissed. The manner in which Coleman had acted was determined to be a case of illegal entrapment. Coleman was admonished by the Court and ordered to return the goods to our company. The compensation for Gaby was that I got him to supervise—yes, supervise—a humiliated Coleman packing the goods for shipment back to our Queensland office.

While these proceedings were taking place, the two Orion companies continued to operate; Orion Systems, with it's ongoing maintenance contracts, and Orion Pet Products by making new inroads into the Australian pet industry. There was no shortage of enthusiastic new customers for Orion Pet Products, especially from the owners of working dogs and from open-minded veterinarians and dog trainers across the country. The expertise and support of those people who earned a living from the care, training, or work of dogs would prove to be very useful in fighting our opponents in the years to come.

In the late 1990s we still gained most of our business directly from the end users, with a few pet shops and vets showing interest in retailing our products. Much of our business was obtained from displaying the products at shows around the country. These included Field Days or country shows at which farmers came to buy a whole range of equipment and supplies which for some was a once a year shopping trip. Most Australian livestock farmers each have a few working dogs and they were quick to recognise that an electronic remote-training collar was a great training tool. Farmers have a much more practical attitude toward livestock and pets than city folk do and they would often be heard to admit that a dog that won't work will soon end up with a bullet in its head. A tool which could help a farmer produce a better working dog was something that was quickly added to the

Field Day shopping list and we never heard any disparagement that the electronic collar could be cruel. In fact, it was always an enjoyable time at the Field Days because the customers were so receptive to our sales message and most of them were eager to test the stimulus given by the collar on themselves and even their wives and children. It became a common trick for one person to activate the collar on their mate's arm, supposedly at the lowest level when they had in fact turned it up to the maximum. Aside from this practical joke, the message from the passers by was always the same: "That wouldn't hurt my dog!"

We also did city shows, focussing more on the containment systems and, at those shows, the message was more about what might happen to their dog without the system—for example, how many dogs are killed on our roads, or how one can stop the dog from digging out those expensive new plants. With those messages, the customer was faced with weighing the decision between what they might think to be an unpleasant sensation to their dog or what the very unpleasant alternative might be. If the result was that the dog owner tried our systems, they would almost immediately become converted to the fact that the collars were both humane and effective.

By the year 2000, we were turning over about $750,000 in business and we had four people working for us, including me and Colleen, who had been made redundant at Neumann Steel. The maintenance contracts at Orion Systems had dwindled to almost zero so we made the hard decision to fold that operation and focus all our attention on Orion Pet Products. Orion Systems had survived for twelve years, from which I had learned a lot, so although it was sad to see its demise, there were many positive attributes about it's existence. It was about this time that we decided to make some changes at Orion Pet Products. We had begun working more closely with the American company and, in order to build the brand name, we decided to change the name of Orion Pet Products to Innotek Australia Pty Ltd. Our thoughts were that perhaps we might build this company over the years to the extent that the American company would want to acquire our operation.

It was during the period, just before 2001, that we started exporting our products when we signed up Roger Jay as our New Zealand distributor and he launched his operation under the name of Innotek NZ, thereby building the brand image across the Tasman Sea. Roger was a one-man band, but one who quickly became a very effective distributor. New Zealand had no laws against our products but, like Australia, pet retailers were reluctant to stock the items because of negative perception about electric shocks. So, Roger concentrated on selling directly to the end user, using direct marketing techniques and by exhibiting at hunting shows and field days.

New Zealand hosts a very large agricultural show at Mystery Creek, near Hamilton, which is probably larger than anything held in Australia. Considering the size of the event, it was quite difficult for Roger to handle the show on his own and so I offered to fly over and help him. I think it was a four day event and we went flat out, from opening to closing time, but I was unable to stay for the last day. We went out for dinner and debated how Roger was going to manage on his own, on the last day of the show. It really was a case of his being unable to take a quick break for a cup of coffee or even to visit the toilet. Something had to be done. I was quite impressed with the waitress who was serving us that evening, so I called her over and asked if she would like some work for the following day. She hesitated and was obviously trying to weigh up what two old guys might have in mind, and whether we could be trusted. We explained what we were looking for and she considered it for a few moments, then said, "Sure, I can do that." In future years, Roger's wife Judy agreed to help him at the Mystery Creek Field Days.

Roger was an unconventional businessman whose lifestyle always came first. During January, Roger lived on his boat and operated via his mobile phone. He stocked up with the most common products and called into coastal towns north of Auckland to ship product to customers from the local post office.

It was at about this time that I was approached by Randy Boyd, the President of Radio Systems Corporation, whose company was the biggest competitor to Innotek in America. He wanted me to switch to his products and although I had purchased a few of his bark collars, I indicated that I was happy with my relationship with Innotek and declined Randy's offer. Many years later, Randy and Radio Systems would come back into my business life.

Lobbying for a change in government regulations was filling a lot of my time at the beginning of the 21st century, both to repeal existing laws against electronic collars, and to ensure that no new restrictions were imposed. We did make some headway following a meeting with the New South Wales Minister for Agriculture. He was quite receptive to our presentation, even though it was quite obvious that the departmental officer at the meeting was trying hard to control the Minister's response. The Minister had never heard of these devices but he was definitely keen to learn more and he asked me to send him videos on the containment system directly to his office. The result was a change to the law in NSW that would allow the use of containment systems but would still ban bark-control collars and remote trainers. A typical political compromise which was introduced to please everyone but probably pleased no one. The strange part is that the containment system generates a larger stimulus than both the bark-control collar and the remote-training collar.

I also made presentations at the federal level and to the state governments of South Australia, Victoria and Queensland. We lobbied the federal government regarding the import restriction on electronic collars and we received a supporting letter from the Minister for Primary Industry but an opposing letter from the Minister for Customs. Obviously there were some dissenting views within this cabinet. The efforts were to bear fruit after a change of government when the import restrictions on electronic collars were eventually removed.

Those import restrictions on electronic collars were the subject of one of the most frightening actions against us, by the authorities. For some time, we had noticed that our shipments were all "red lined" by Australian Customs. This meant that they were subject to long delays while the Customs searched through all of our shipments. No doubt they had been directed to look for a device with a collar attached in which case they could take action against us. It does make you wonder how an independent charity like the RSPCA could have such control over a department of the Federal Government. They finally found something they could act upon. We had two shipments sent out from the Innotek factory in Fort Wayne, Indiana, one with collars and the other with electronics. It so happened that some diligent employee of Expeditors, the freight company, spotted the two shipments in the freight company's warehouse in Indianapolis and decided he would save the company some money by consolidating the two shipments. Later the freight company's employees in Expeditor's Brisbane office would notice the consolidation and knowing the way in which we imported these separate shipments, they proceeded to un-consolidate them.

Somehow the Customs authorities found out about this particular shipment after the delivery was compete. Unable to intercept the shipment, they decided this was a serious enough situation to apply for, and obtain, search warrants for Innotek's and the Expeditor's offices. Seven Federal Customs officers and Australian Federal Police (AFP) descended on our office, one morning, while another team of eight brave officers was swooping down on the freight office in Brisbane. Badges were flashed, recording devices were set up, and employees were warned that any comments they made would be taken down and could be used as evidence against them. These turkeys had been watching too many Hollywood movies.

The raid took place while I was visiting Colleen in hospital and I became aware of it only after Jamie, my operations manager, called me to say that the office was full of police. The senior police officer was put on the line and I asked, firstly, for them to allow Jamie to fax the search warrant to my solicitor and, secondly, for them to wait until I could return to the office from the hospital. When those requests were refused, I asked the officer to record my requests and note down the refusal. I was then asked to hold the line and, after a short time, the officer came back to say they would wait. Sometimes, it's best to stand up to such people.

When I arrived at the office, I immediately faxed the warrant to my solicitor and went outside to call him on my mobile phone. I then went back into my office and witnessed uniformed officers searching through files and some even with plastic gloves, going through the garbage. An AFP's computer specialist was struggling to access our computer files and, when I asked him if he had a problem, he said he didn't know anything about Apple computers. Let us hope, for the sake of our nation's security, that things have improved in the Australian Federal Police's computer department, since then.

When I found out what the investigation was all about, it was easy enough to give them the information they were looking for about the shipment in question. They wanted to know if we could identify the inventory in question. That was not possible, since the items do not carry serial numbers, but Jamie was able to inform me that a number of remote training collars in that shipment had been sold to the Queensland Police for their dog squad. I suggested that the officers might like to raid the Queensland Police stations and confiscate the collars they were using. The whole situation was beginning to look rather farcical.

After the SWAT team had left us and we had all calmed down, I decided to get some assistance from authorities who might support us. I made a submission to the Ombudsman, I contacted our local Member of Parliament, and I got in touch with the United States Department of Commerce to ask for their assistance, since this was about American goods being legally imported into Australia. I knew that things would not be resolved quickly but I had no concern that we could possibly lose from this. If they pursued the matter and the press got hold of this story, Federal Customs and the Australian Federal Police would look like a pack of fools. In fact, about six months later, we were informed that the investigation had been dropped. No further explanation was given and none was expected.

The poor guys at Expeditors were not taking things so lightly however. The Customs officers had alleged that they had been fraudulent in changing the documents, and this could result in jail terms. I heard, some time later, that one of their employees was on the verge of a nervous breakdown. It looked like a repeat of poor old Gaby's predicament, when he had planned to leave the country—all of this, over dog collars.

So far, we had beaten the RSPCA in New South Wales, we had persuaded the NSW government to amend a law in our favour, and now we had withstood a savage attack from the Customs authorities. The RSPCA decided to escalate their campaign against us in the media. In Queensland, the Chief of Staff at Channel 9 purchased a containment system, supposedly for his dog and, within a few days, the Chief Inspector at the RSPCA was shown holding the collar on Channel 9 News, declaring it to be cruel and calling out for these collars to be banned. The next week, the containment system was returned for a refund and, when I refused, I was threatened by the chap at Channel 9 that he would ruin me. My solicitor advised me to refund the guy's money, which I did. Recently, the Manager in question resigned from Channel 9 having been caught fabricating a story about reporting from a crime site when he, the reporter, was in fact sitting in the Channel 9 helicopter at their base. Not a good look for the profession of journalism.

The next attack was a two pronged one from Victoria. A headline story in Melbourne's Herald Sun purported to show how one of our collars had "burned" the arm of the Melbourne inspector. That picture was later shown to have been fabricated. On the same day, Channel 9's television program, A Current Affair, did an exposé of the cruel electronic collar industry and how they were sold "undercover." They called on one of our resellers, without saying who they were, masquerading as a potential customer, but carrying a hidden camera. The poor quality of the image made it look as if there were some kind of subterfuge going on. The background to the story indicated that these devices had to be sold undercover because there was something illegal about them. This was backed up by the President of the RSPCA claiming they were illegal. What he meant was that they were an illegal import if imported complete, although he didn't say that.

Our requests for a rebuttal fell on deaf ears. We would simply spoil the story if we could show that these were beneficial products, both effective and humane. The story said that we were the bad guys and presenting any contrary information would just end any chance of the newspaper or TV station running follow-up stories. The Brisbane Courier Mail and Channel 7's Today Tonight followed with more horror stories, all emanating from the RSPCA.

I was now beginning to feel that I had picked a fight with a huge and powerful organisation and I was starting to question whether this was all that wise. I was not the first person in my family to take on powerful enemies, I found out. Separate to these events, I have become interested in researching my family tree and, according to the records of the Mormon Church, I am descended from the Reverend John Rogers. John Rogers was born in England, educated at Cambridge, and became the Rector of the Holy Trinity Church in the City of London. In 1534, he moved to Antwerp where he joined Protestant reformers and so became an enemy of the most powerful organisation of the time, the Roman Catholic Church. Upon returning to England, in 1548, he proceeded to preach against popery, idolatry and superstition. Unfortunately this was the time when Queen Mary (Bloody Mary), a Catholic monarch, came to the throne, so John Rogers had some powerful enemies indeed. In fact, he lost his fight and, on 4 February 1555, he was taken to Smithfield Market, in London, where he was burned at the stake.

At the time, I didn't know about John Rogers. Thus, I couldn't conclude that an inherited trait was driving me to fight powerful organisations. We spoke to so many experts, but got no advice on how to go about fighting this ongoing persecution. A professor at Bond University, a specialist in public relations, shook his head and concluded, "I'm sorry. I don't think there is anything you can do in this situation. The RSPCA are just too strong." One person did give me hope for a defence, however, and that was our lawyer, Paul Everingham. He said that we could fight them in the courts but he warned us that it would be a very tough fight, which we might not win; and, if we lost, we would probably lose everything. It was a very sobering warning but it did bring into sharp focus our options. We thought about it long and hard. The alternative was worse. In response to the public's outrage at the stories about the collars which could "burn dogs' necks," the politicians would have introduced total bans against our products, and the RSPCA would have succeeded in closing us down.

We had to go into battle. What followed, was the drama you have already read in this book's opening chapter.

Toughing It Out

been in paramount legal action before, and became the Recorder of the said Thirty Places in the Diocese of London in 1631. He looked to advocate where he found Protestant scholars and scholastic elements of the most prominent organization of the time. He became well aware that the Scottish rising in England in 1639. He once read a speech at his funeral delivered and eulogized him. Strangely they also was the same who is Oxford Mary Ulloa New York. Catholic monarch came to the throne. Sir John Rogers and some powerful sell me to bed. In fact, he lost his fight and up a Archbishop saying he was glad to South their matter. In truth, he shows he was turned at the stake.

For the first grade group about four hundred. Thus, I conclude...and despatched up the grip was drawing me to high pitch of up himself. We agreed that many experts, but yet the strategy is how to go about talking this or doing it necessarily. A professor at Boul University... speakable in public volumes a shook his head and concluded, "You won't, I don't think there is anything you can do in this situation. The USPCA's view that 170 about." The present bill gave me hope in a definite; however, and that was the kind of the threshold. He said they weren't a high bar in the...bird. I would have told how old he was even if he'd been. What I'm might not have and, there for, we would probably lose everything. It was a very sobering meeting but if but come into things took out of hand. We thought about it long and hard. The alternative was worse. In response to distribute outrageous the charity, then the college's when could I burn digest body of the charity, and the introduced third thinking against our problem; and the RSPCA bill have succeeded in closing us down.

We had to go into battle, Whatever the outcome, the drama you have already read in this book's one, one one chapter.

162

CHAPTER 18

GOING SOLAR

By 2003, we were outgrowing our small Mudgeeraba office and looking for alternatives. I had studied potential building sites with the thought that I should build our own office in the area, but no suitable building land became available which the city council would zone for commercial use. In the end we decided to sign a lease on an office unit which was under construction nearby. The unit was one of four in an attractive complex with ample parking and easy access to the highway. It was perfect for our requirements and would have been just the kind of structure we would have built had we been fortunate enough to find a suitable location.

The problem (and the opportunity) was that the builder was running into financial problems and found it difficult to meet the Council's demands on landscaping the property. I liked the builder and I thought that he had done a fabulous job, so I proposed a method by which he could finish the construction and landscaping, thereby gaining a completion certificate from Council. The offer was to advance him 12 months rental to cover his shortfall, which would allow him to complete the building. In return we would receive an option to purchase the building at an agreed price should he be unable to finalise the loans required for him to continue as the landlord. His problem became our opportunity and as a result, together with another prospective tenant, we formed the Worongary Business Park Trust, in which we owned 80% and the other tenant had 20%. Later we bought out the minority partner and owned the Worongary Business Park outright.

I think this demonstrates the opportunities that become available once a business becomes profitable and is generating a positive cash flow. We could have taken the profits and excess cash out of Innotek and perhaps bought a bigger house, or a yacht, but we decided to reinvest the income in another business. I have found that opportunities regularly present themselves, provided you are vigilant about what is going on around you and provided that you have some capital available to invest. I had seen a number of similar opportunities in the past, but this was the first time that I was in a position to act upon it.

Now, seven years later, the Worongary Business Park is still fully leased and bringing greater profits than I could get with a bank or an investment fund. Having found the right property, I am now sold on the idea of investing in commercial real estate. In fact the Trust has since gone on to buy another industrial property across the street from the Worongary Business Park, plus a residential unit in Mudgeeraba.

I continue to hold that life is one, long networking event. To prove my point, consider the Canadian holiday that Colleen and I took, in 2004. I managed to make contact with my old friend Dave Lay from my IBM Canada days. He was living in Vancouver and after I called him up he invited me out to dinner. He told me about his early retirement from IBM and his unsuccessful attempts at a couple of business ventures which cost him his retirement funds and almost made him bankrupt. Before going completely broke, he and his wife split the remaining funds and he invested his share in the stock market. Just as this had proven successful for him at IBM, he had not forgotten his investing skills. Reverting to what he did best ultimately proved very successful for him in retirement and he and his wife Verna were now quite financially secure.

Upon hearing about my successes in setting up distributorships for various products in Australia, he suggested that I should contact a company in which he was a significant investor. That company was Carmanah Technologies, Inc. of Victoria, British Columbia, a developer and manufacturer of solar-powered LED (light-emitting diode) lights. They had developed some cutting-edge solar-powered beacons for marine and aviation applications, which had been widely accepted by coast guard and defence organisations in North America and Europe. Dave had hit a chord with this one and I quizzed him for as much information as he could supply, determined to pursue the opportunity as soon as I got home.

A string of emails, telephone calls and letters later, I identified an opportunity for someone to represent Carmanah in Australia. Various organisations had made attempts at selling some of Carmanah's products into specific vertical markets in Australia but none had been really successful. The big question from Carmanah was why I should be any different, so the first thing they asked me to do was put together a business plan.

I realised that I could not set up and run another business while I still had Innotek to run, but I did see that I could direct a new company if I had someone I could trust to run it. That's when I approached my son, Richard. He had been selling cars for Toyota, doing quite well, but I felt that he might be looking for other opportunities. Richard was keen, so he became the lynch pin for the business plan of our new venture, Orion Solar Pty Ltd. A date was set to visit Victoria, BC and nail down an agreement or at least get Carmanah's commitment to give us time to prove ourselves. At the end of September 2004, Richard and I flew to Victoria for meetings with the CEO and various division managers at Carmanah.

The meetings were successful and Richard returned to Australia to hand in his notice and start working on our new venture. The big difference between this business and previous ventures of mine was the fact that Innotek had a great cash flow and was in a good position to fund another start-up. Also I could set up Richard's operation in the corner of our office and share all of the administration costs. It was a perfect opportunity to launch a new business venture without worrying about how to pay the bills.

Orion Solar hit the ground running, with a display at the annual conference and exhibition of the Australian Airports Association, in Alice Springs, in November, 2004. Carmanah managed to get us enough aviation lights to display at the show and we made contact with our first prospects. We and our products were well received at the AAA Show but we were faced with more uncertainty in the form of the ubiquitous government regulations. If there is a different way of doing things from the rest of the world, then the various Australian governments will find a way. I suppose we should have expected this, especially when you consider the safety aspects of aviation. For Orion Solar, the solution was not in trying to change the regulations but in learning what they were and how we could work around them. For the aviation market, this meant targeting the remote airfields which did not service aircraft carrying 15 or more passengers.

Learning from our relationship with Epic Data, we organised an official launch of Orion Solar in cooperation with the Canadian Consulate in Sydney. Their office is near Circular Quay, with a 5th-floor patio which overlooks the Sydney Harbour Bridge and the Opera House. This was a perfect location for making a good first impression on anyone who came to our launch. We compiled a guest list in cooperation with the Consular staff and an embossed invitation from the Consulate General was sent to all our prospects. Bruce Edgar, our Sales Representative from Carmanah, came from Canada for the function and we set up a display of the entire Carmanah line, including marine, aviation, transportation and general illumination products. Having loosened the guests with Moosehead beer and Canadian wines, the function went over well and the good ship "Orion Solar" was launched without a hitch.

Following the launch, Richard, Bruce and I set up an exhibit at the Australian International Air show, at Avalon, with Richard and Bruce taking a side trip to Canberra to make a presentation to the Airfield Lighting Engineers. We kept Bruce busy during his visit to Australia and he was a great help to us.

Carmanah has not been the easiest of suppliers to deal with. During the time we have been selling their products, Carmanah has gone through three CEOs and three sales managers. They have also diversified into and out of several different businesses, including edge-lit signs, lighting for bus stops and bus shelters, and grid tied systems. They have remained in marine lighting, even though they merged some products and distribution outlets with Sabik, a Finnish manufacturer. In aviation lighting, they made similar streamlining arrangements with ADB, a Belgian airfield lighting manufacturer. During these changes, some of Carmanah's management recommended unfavourable changes to our distribution arrangements, which we have successfully countered. During this period, Carmanah's share prices have slumped from over $3.50 to around 50 cents a share.

I conclude that a distribution agreement is only as good as the supplier and the products offered. In the high-risk area of a business based on new technology, a potential threat to the distributor is the possibility of the supplier ceasing business. In order to minimise this risk, we have attempted to diversify our product range by finding additional suppliers and by developing our own products. Finding additional suppliers has not been easy because of the unique nature of the products we are selling, but we have made progress in developing our own solar light controller.

Orion Solar has been slow to reach a stage where the business could stand on its own and this is largely due to the fact that we were introducing a new technology, rather than supplying something which is tried and tested. Any new business needs capital to cover a sometimes lengthy period until the regular sales have reached a level beyond breakeven point.

Orion Solar has reached that stage with its current level of overheads and has now grown independent of its parent, Innotek Australia. In fact, in 2011, Orion moved to their own warehouse and office space in a building purchased by the Worongary Business Park Trust.

CHAPTER 19

GIVING BACK

I MENTIONED MY INTEREST in genealogy and the links I had discovered with ancestors like John Rogers, the martyr. This fascination with the subject was prompted by the knowledge that a recent ancestor of mine was the Reverend Walter Henry Medhurst. Medhurst was quite a famous missionary with the London Missionary Society who had spent many years in the Far East and was one of three men responsible for translating the Bible into Chinese. As a child, growing up with my maternal grandfather, I was aware of this ancestor and our house was filled with various artefacts that Medhurst's family had brought back to England from China. My mother always spoke of her grandmother who she said, was born in China.

The advent of the Internet allowed me to find out more about Walter Henry Medhurst and, once I opened that door, it was like stepping into another world. I discovered that Medhurst, who had completed an apprenticeship to become a master printer, was recruited by the London Missionary Society to set up a press at the LMS's new station in Malacca, in what is today peninsular Malaysia. Described as being of "wiry frame, good health and unfailing cheerfulness," the 20-year-old Medhurst left London on August 30, 1816 for the ten-month journey to his new home. During a three-month stopover in Madras, India, he was hosted by Mr. and Mrs. William Loveless, who were also missionaries with the LMS. It was at this time that he met and married

Elizabeth Braune who was staying with the Loveless family as governess to their children. Though only twenty-two years old, Elizabeth was already a widow having had two children, one of which had died. Walter Medhurst and Elizabeth were married on 19 May, 1817 and they set sail the following day for Malacca.

The Medhursts spent five years in Malacca and Walter was himself ordained before taking up a mission in Batavia (now Jakarta, Indonesia). My great-grandmother was in fact born in Batavia, and not in China, as Mum had said. Medhurst lived in Batavia for twenty-one years where he founded his English Church, which still operates today as the All Saints Anglican Church, close to the centre of modern day Jakarta. I also discovered that Medhurst had founded the Parapattan Orphanage in Batavia in the year 1832 and, unbelievably, it is still operating today.

I decided that fate wanted me to get involved with my great-great grandfather's legacy. We were doing well in business and I had developed skills which could be applied to helping an organisation like Parapattan. Perhaps it was time to give something back. Through the Internet, I had linked up with Jakarta-based Thomas Bergstrom, an American missionary who had ties with Parapattan through his role with Family Care Indonesia. He indicated that although Parapattan was extremely well run, they could always use some assistance with a number of projects. Thomas was to introduce me to the directors of the orphanage and they invited me to visit them in Jakarta if that was possible.

We had been trying to develop business for Innotek, in Indonesia, so it was an opportune time to visit Jakarta. As a result, in April 2008, Colleen and I arranged to spend a week in Indonesia which would include a visit to Parapattan and the All Saints Church. To maximise our efforts in developing our future business prospects, we secured the support of Austrade to help us find a suitable distributor. Although our products were not manufactured in Australia our role as the regional distributor made us eligible for Austrade's support. As a result, we set up appointments with four potential distributors and Austrade supplied us with a car, a driver, and translator for visits around Jakarta. This support was invaluable and showed what a beneficial resource government trade agencies can be when trying to develop exports.

In spite of this support, we were not particularly successful in Indonesia, a predominantly Islamic country. Dogs are not popular pets, so the market is limited to non-Muslims and expatriates living in Indonesia. Furthermore, the average income is low, so our products were attractive only to wealthier people. But wealthier people had servants, whose job it was to look after the dogs, so a containment system or an anti-barking collar was largely unnecessary. Add to these factors the fact that we were introducing a completely new product, and it is easy to see why our market was less than receptive. One needs to learn more about a foreign market before trying to introduce a product in that environment. Going back there, today, with our expanded product line, many of which are attractive to cat owners—and cats are time-honoured pets in Muslim cultures—would probably represent a better opportunity in the Indonesian market.

I also investigated potential projects which could support Parapattan. Looking at the possibility of fund raising within Australia, I had Rotary in mind as a potential partner and I wanted to have a story to present to Australian Rotary Clubs when I returned. I was aware of funds being available through Rotary International in situations which involved Rotary Clubs in two countries. For this reason, I made a presentation to the Rotary Club of Jakarta about my interest in supporting one of their local orphanages. Since the Rotary Club was my first meeting in Jakarta I could only outline the reasons for my visit and conceptualise my ideas for what might happen. I was extremely well received and gained interesting feedback from those in attendance but as it turned out I was not going to need their support after all. A significant memory however, was meeting with a Rotarian who was an architect and as a child was abandoned to an orphanage by his parents because he was physically handicapped. He told me that the orphanage enabled him to achieve success in his life beyond anything that would have been possible with his family. That was quite an amazing statement.

Our next visit was to the All Saints Anglican Church, which is the oldest English institution in Jakarta and is attended mainly by expatriates and embassy staff. Here, we found references to the founder and the memorial stone to Sarah, the eldest daughter of Walter and Eliza Medhurst. Sarah was married in 1836 to the Reverend Henry Lockwood, a missionary colleague of her father's, when she was just 16. Shortly afterwards her parents and younger siblings left for an extended trip to England. Sarah died within six months of their leaving. The harshness of that era is underlined by her younger brother's death from scarlet fever, soon after the family arrived back in England. The Medhursts returned to Batavia in 1838 and my great-grandmother, Augusta, was born there in 1840.

The following day, we met for lunch with the directors and senior staff of the Parapattan Orphanage. The directors were mostly well educated, professional or business people. They jokingly told me that I looked just like my ancestor, whose picture appears in an overview of the orphanage. We heard all about the celebrations for the 175th birthday of the orphanage which had taken place the year before and they wished that they had met me then because we could have been honoured guests. Thomas, the American missionary, and his wife Katrina also joined us at lunch. As indicated by Thomas, our meeting confirmed his view that Parapattan was a well managed orphanage.

Afterwards, we tackled the crazy Jakarta traffic to travel across town to the orphanage itself. Located fairly close to the centre of this sprawling city, Parapattan moved to their current location in 1958, this being the third location since their founding in 1832. The facility consists of a two story building used for administration plus common areas like indoor play room, storage and kitchens. It was in this building that they had allocated space for a planned library and sick dispensary. An outdoor, covered patio is used as a dining area and accommodation blocks are located behind a large playing field. A basketball hoop was on their wish list for the playing field.

At the time of our visit, Parapattan had about 65 children originating from all over Indonesia. All attend private Christian schools in the area. This adds considerably to the cost of their education but, from all reports, many of the children are scoring very highly in their courses and doing well. The children's ages range between four and eighteen and there was an even mix of boys and girls.

After the tour, we gathered in the dining area where it was explained who we were and my connection with the founder of the institution was revealed. I was asked to say a few words to the children and one of the senior girls translated into Indonesian. Finally, the children's choir sang for us and I found it hard to fight back the tears. We had come with small clip-on koalas for each of the children but we left with a desire to give them something much more enduring after our return home.

The directors had outlined their plans for a library and a sick bay/dispensary and, after getting some quotations emailed to us, we saw that Innotek Australia could easily afford to cover the cost of this project without having to organise a fund raising campaign targeting outside organisations. The project was completed and the new library has been designated The Medhurst Library. Thomas was able to monitor the work, even though we could rely on the competence of the directors. For his trouble, we transferred an extra ten per cent of the funds for him to allocate to the charities of his choice.

We later sent further funds to Parapattan to purchase gifts for the children at Christmas. Our staff at the warehouse raised money on their own initiative, to donate to the orphanage's Christmas fund, by selling recycled scrap cartons on eBay. So, the children did get their wished-for basketball hoop, and a pool table, and a fussball game.

CHAPTER 20

✳

AIMING TO BE THE BEST

IN OUR ACROSS-THE-BOARD EFFORTS to achieve business excellence, I would constantly enter the companies that I owned in various business award competitions. Each of our award entries was an exercise that made us consider every aspect of the business, required us to write a business plan, and drove us to examine our strengths and weaknesses. Merely competing for an award was a benefit to our operation and the more employees and outside advisors we engaged in the task, the greater was the overall benefit. I still have copies of those award entries, over the years, and they still make good reading on how the company operated and succeeded at the time.

Twice, we were State Finalists in the Telstra Business Awards competition and the gala dinner of that event became a great reward for our key employees. I recall one junior employee claiming that the night of the Telstra Business Awards was the best night of his life. I think his claim was a reflection of the quiet life this young man led, but it was rewarding to know how he felt. I always felt we were winners, despite the actual awards outcomes. I believe that the announced winners are picked largely for the story that the contest organisers can use to promote future awards, rather than as a measure of how successfully the business was run. Hence, stories about people starting businesses from their kitchen table always upstaged stories about carefully crafted business plans. I don't harbour any grudges against entries like that because, each time we entered the race for an award, it sharpened our business sense and was a lot of fun.

One fellow who comes to mind for his success story, rather than for the substance of his business, was the winner who beat us at the Gold Coast Business Awards. He was the owner of the Mount Tamborine Distillery and he turned up at the black-tie dinner dressed as Santa Claus in shorts and a Hawaiian shirt. He beat us, hands down, on showmanship and made us look like a bunch of boring bankers.

I seized other ways to keep our company ahead of the competition by using the services of a business coach. Coaches vary widely in effectiveness and influence. George Bernard Shaw once said, "He who can, does. He who cannot, teaches." I have known clueless coaches, but occasionally one comes across someone with the right talent. I found a coach who had developed good systems for managing both the coaching process and the goals, strategies and daily activities of the client. He was very dedicated and hard working and had a good way of getting me to reach decisions by probing and suggesting, rather than by telling me what he would do. We set up one hour each week for a telephone conversation at which we would discuss ways of handling various activities in the business. These discussions would cover everything from short- and long-term goals, to daily activities related to sales, customer service and human resources.

One of the skills I developed from this coaching was to better manage staff and weed out the non-performers. In one case, I had the chance to advance someone to a more senior position but the obvious candidate was in an easy job and I seriously doubted whether he was prepared for the hard work required. During the coaching session, we discussed a way of putting this forward to the candidate so that he would see it as a promotion, but be fully aware that the easy times of his current job would end. I told the candidate that I was in no rush for a decision and gave him a couple of weeks to think about it. This strategy worked because, in less than two weeks, he announced that he was moving on to another opportunity. We were able to find a more suitable candidate and filled this position with a more junior person, and we didn't need to terminate anyone.

Perhaps one of our best business improvement activities was our Friday-afternoon-drink session. The results were equal to or better than anything a management consultant could offer. We would open the bar at 4:30 p.m. and invite our team to imbibe and generously unwind from the week's toils. This invariably caused the staff to review the week's events and, with a small amount of alcohol, tongues loosened and ideas flowed. These sessions rarely went to more than one or two drinks, but that was enough to get even the quietest employees to come up with ideas. One change in the way we did business, coming out of a Friday session, was the decision to sell spray collars. Previously, we had offered only static bark collars for unruly dogs, based on the notion that static collars were far more effective at stopping nuisance barking than spray collars. What we had failed to see was that a lot of dog owners wanted to buy spray collars in preference to static collars, which meant that we were not giving customers what they wanted. It was such a basic business error and one that we had overlooked. It took a couple of stubbies of beer on a Friday afternoon and the problem was solved.

Medhurst in conversation with Choo-Tih-Lang. 1838

CHAPTER 21

*

THREAT MEETS OPPORTUNITY

FIVE YEARS AFTER WE had fought and won our case against the Royal Society for the Prevention of Cruelty to Animals, our company and the industry in which we operated was flourishing. If we were not the market leader within our industry, we were close to it. We had certainly pioneered the industry and our supplier from America, Invisible Technologies, was equal in size and success to their competitor, Radio Systems, owner of the PetSafe brand of electronic dog collars. The Australian distributor for PetSafe was one of Australia's largest distributors of pet products, Kramar Pet Products. They had done very little to promote this category of pet product in our industry but they had been very skilful at getting pet retailers to adopt the products which we had found so difficult in our early years. Kramar sales people would tell me that they loved it when we ran national advertising for our products because it stimulated the demand which they would be able to fill through their retail network. This outcome did not seem fair, but we were doing well and there was plenty of room for everyone.

The next bombshell to hit us at Innotek came on September 13, 2006. I was wearing my Orion hat at the time, working at a Marine Safety Show with Richard, when Zane Rice, our sales rep from Innotek, called to say that the US company had been purchased by arch rival, Radio Systems Corporation. The message came like a punch to the midriff. Zane did not know what would happen as a result, and the public announcement wasn't made until a few days later. Pessimists would be quick to point out that we would probably lose the Innotek range of products and that Kramar would be taking over the distributorship. After all Kramar was one of the largest pet distributors in Australia and financed by AMP Private Equity, plus the relationship between Radio Systems and Kramar was already well established and that was a factor which would be hard to challenge.

I always think that every problem has the potential to be turned around into an opportunity. I refused to allow myself to think that we could lose everything after building the business and the industry over all these years. We had pioneered this industry and we had built a team of people and resellers to supply and support the products throughout Australia and New Zealand. I considered that our company was the perfect partner for Radio Systems. After reviewing the options and comparing the strengths and weaknesses of our company, versus Kramar, I was absolutely convinced that we were by far the best choice for Radio Systems in choosing representation in this region.

Within hours of receiving what seemed like devastating news, I knew that I had to get an appointment with Randy Boyd, President of Radio Systems, to share with him my vision of Innotek Australia as the regional distributor for all his products. The public announcement of the acquisition was dated 16 September and I emailed him a letter of congratulations on 18 September, including an expression of interest in doing more for Radio Systems in Australia. Unfortunately, my enthusiasm to arrange a meeting as soon as possible did not match the time pressures faced by Randy Boyd in his efforts to merge these two large companies in America. Often in business, I have found, once I had the seed of an idea, it was quite difficult to slow down to meet the realism under which development of the idea was possible. It was a case of developing patience. Over the next few weeks it became apparent that some of the Invisible Technologies people would not be staying on and others would be moved into the RSC operation. Innotek's European sales representative, Titch White, was assigned to help existing Innotek customers merge into the new operation and he ultimately took over as our main contact. Having had previous contact with Randy Boyd was an advantage and they were receptive to a meeting. So it was that, on December 5, I rocked up to Electric Avenue in Knoxville, Tennessee to meet our new partners.

Having a few weeks to prepare for this meeting turned out to be of major significance. I put together the most comprehensive picture of our company, our market and our vision for the future. I projected several scenarios to show what we would do depending upon how much of RSC's business we could count on within our region. In preparing my presentation I was constantly thinking that someone at Kramar was doing the same for their company and I was determined to be better than them. As it turned out I don't think they bothered to even ask the question. I think they assumed that they would automatically take over all of RSC's products. In hindsight it was easy to see how complacent Kramar had become when I understood how they perceived of us as a little company, hardly more than a home business. We would show them that we were much more than that.

I had allowed for two days in Knoxville, and it was good that I had, because the meetings went well and I was asked to come back for further discussions. I was very impressed with Randy and his team, thinking that I should have cemented a relationship with Radio Systems, when Randy had first approached me, in the late-1990s. It was not too late, however, and I came away from the meetings reassured that we would continue to have exclusivity on all of the products we were currently buying and that RSC would consider Innotek as their Australian distributor on other products. We had placed ourselves in an excellent position to move forward. A negative had been turned into a positive.

I came back to Australia feeling high about the future and was able to paint an exciting prospect for our staff members. They responded with great enthusiasm, pledging to beat Kramar out in the market and planning for every possibility of taking over some of their products. We had not been offered the full product range but we could plan for it should the situation arise. We had previously purchased components only from Invisible Technologies, and RSC wanted to ship us complete SKUs, direct from China, so there were quite a few changes to be implemented. We took the initiative of contacting RSC's China office and, in March, 2007, Jamie and I flew to Shenzhen to meet with Tim Behling and Howard Fehl and visit some of their factories. Different supply and logistics functions have since been put in place and we would not now have had this direct contact with China, but at the time it was beneficial and helped position us as the exclusive distributor for Australia.

It was October, 2007 before we would progress further with the RSC relationship. Brad van der Veen, Clay Odom and Titch White visited Australia to discuss how we would take over the distribution of all RSC products in Australia and New Zealand, including the supply to existing distributors such as Brooklands and Kramar. The guys had already visited Kramar in Sydney to break the news to them. For Innotek, this meant that new challenges had been put before us in the form of a doubling of product lines and taking on the supply of our former competitor. Supplying Kramar would be a challenge because they were not receptive to the idea and we would have to win them over.

Jamie and I travelled to Sydney the following week to meet with Kramar's CEO and to sell them on the level of support we would provide. The sensitive issue revolved around how we would prevent our sales force from soliciting Kramar's accounts. Our solution was for Kramar to use our people as sales support, involving them with Kramar's sales force and their customers and by doing so allow relationships to develop. The most likely result was that any conflict would be ironed out at the sales level but, if not, we would intervene to have Innotek back off from any sale. Agreement was reached and a follow-up plan discussed.

Jamie and our sales manager, Megan, returned to Sydney the next week to meet with the Kramar sales team and commence some training. That is where things started to go wrong. The attendees at the meeting were limited to a few head office personnel and Jamie was warned that several topics would be off the discussion agenda. It was obvious that someone was trying to sabotage our efforts.

This meeting was indicative of what followed and, although we did supply Kramar for about a year after this, the sales volumes were in decline and they were obviously not committed to making the relationship work. It ended, in 2009, when Kramar launched a competitive range of products, a move which confirmed they were not sincere in working with us right from the start.

Could we have handled the situation any differently, so that Kramar would continue to sell our products? I think there was nothing further we could do. They were like a Premier League football team that had been beaten by amateurs and were now being told that they would be coached by the team that beat them.

The following three years were good for Innotek Australia. With a steady growth in sales and profits, the company increased it's market share and was able to successfully take over and support the retail stores formerly supplied by Kramar. Kramar's new product line failed in the market, as we had expected it to, largely because of their inability to provide the necessary technical support. The nature of our business changed, with more sales through reseller channels and less direct sales to the end user. This meant that our sales message had to change; we now had to regularly call on retailers and come up with new point-of-sale and promotional ideas. There was a lot to learn about how large retail chains do business with their suppliers, but we found that most organisations were quite easy to deal with. For me, the pet industry was easy-going and laid back, compared to my previous experience in information technology.

Downsizing our end-user business was not so good from a cash flow position because end-users paid cash up front, but since we were funnelling our increased profits into the company, the result was that our banking position moved from overdraft to cash surplus and the value of the company surged. The healthy position of Innotek Australia meant that we could support the growth of Orion Solar, and we were able to buy out the balance of the Worongary Business Park Trust.

During this period, I contracted with various outside consultants to assist us in developing new plans for building and diversifying the company. This was probably the first time in my business career that I owned a business which had become established and which would continue to operate successfully even in my absence. It gave me more time to sit back and plan. We applied for and were granted government support for increasing employment and we entered local and national business awards, on several occasions being selected as finalists. All of these activities required us to spell out our business plans, including mission statements and visions of where we wanted to be in the future. This last question of where we wanted to be in the future was of special significance to me personally and started me thinking about an exit plan.

At about this time, a flyer arrived in the mail promoting a seminar at Bond University on the subject of "Developing an Exit Strategy." The message was that the post-World War II Baby Boomers were reaching retirement age and, as a result, there would soon be a glut of businesses on the market from these "wanna be" retirees. It would take time to prepare and sell a business and the message was that business owners should plan for that eventuality well ahead of time.

I reviewed the lessons of the seminar and set about improving some of the systems and records of the company so that I would have a tidied-up business to offer any potential buyer. I thought about the leverage which would make my business of greater value to certain buyers because of the strategic value that we could offer. I thought it would be a good idea to contact a business broker to see what he thought about my business and what steps I ought to take in planning for a future sale.

On the Internet, I found what I thought was the website of a helpful broker and I keyed in an enquiry on their online form in the expectation that a salesman would contact me. But I had inadvertently made the enquiry on the site of the national association of business brokers, so the message went out to all their members around Australia. The Internet can be really good for fast communication but it can be really bad if you get it wrong.

I was inundated with responses from every business broker from Cairns to Tasmania and these guys are some of the best sales people going. Fortunately, they did turn out to be fairly discreet when calling the office. The biggest challenge now was how I could turn some of them off which ultimately I did. In the process, I compiled a large file on business brokers and where I could use them in my exit strategy. In summary I resolved that I would probably be better off doing the work myself, targeting potential buyers based on the argument that we might be a good strategic partner for them. That might include another distributor looking to expand, an overseas company wanting to set up in Australia, or a business migrant looking for a successful business. In all those cases the purchaser would be spending money to do something else in addition to buying the business at its agreed value. That something else might persuade them to pay more for the business than would be achieved by a listing through a broker.

At one stage, I thought we had a buyer for our company when we were approached by a business broker from New Zealand, supposedly with an office in China, who claimed to have someone interested in purchasing the company. They said that they could not divulge the name of the interested party, only that they were from China and they were interested in buying the business as part of the Australian government's Business Migration Program. This sounded feasible. They asked me to name a price, which I did with a bit of padding and to my surprise they came back to say that the price was acceptable. They asked me to have a Heads of Agreement drawn up which I did and the people from New Zealand confirmed that it was acceptable but that it would have to be translated into Chinese. Furthermore they said that they had someone who could do the translation for $1,500. Coincidentally, I had just returned from China where I had been on a trade mission involving Orion Solar. Austrade had arranged for one of their translators to accompany us on various factory visits and I had kept her business card. I decided to ask her if she could translate the agreement for us, which she did for about $100.

The Chinese translation of the Heads of Agreement was emailed to the broker in New Zealand and we eagerly awaited the response from the Chinese buyer. That was the last we heard from our purported business broker. It appears now that the whole thing was a scam, intended to embezzle the cost of translation from us. A few phone calls later, I found out that other Queensland businesses had been deceived in the same way and a friend of one of my staff had paid $2,000 for non-existent translation services. It seems that they went to a lot of trouble for a small amount of money but who knows how many companies they swindled.

The experience was just one example of the many scams that the average businessman has to face from time to time. And many of these are much more sophisticated than the typical consumer scam, such as those emails one receives from Nigeria, asking you to help share in millions. I did report this incident to the Australian Securities and Investment Commission through their web page that solicits people to report scams. I did not receive a response, so I think the lesson is caveat emptor and don't rely on the government to protect you.

Colleen and John receiving a Telstra Business Award

CHAPTER 22

*

END GAME

It had been more than three years since I had visited Knoxville to present the idea that we should become the exclusive distributor for Radio Systems, although I had met with Randy at the InterZoo Show in Nuremberg, Germany in 2008. I continue to believe that selling our suppliers and keeping them onside is just as important as selling to our customers. Neglecting to visit Radio Systems during this period was totally against this philosophy. So, a visit was planned for June of 2010, which would precede our normal annual holidays including a visit to Canada.

We discussed with Titch the topics that we would like to cover while in Knoxville and the people we would like to meet with. During the period since we first became the RSC distributor, a number of new companies had been acquired, including Premier Pet Products, Vet Ventures and the Pet Porte microchip cat door, so there were plenty of subjects to cover. Titch casually mentioned that while I was in Knoxville, the subject might come up of whether I would be interested in selling Innotek to Radio Systems. Bingo!

That sentence was all I heard about preparing for our June visit. June 14 had suddenly become the day of opportunity on which I could climax my whole involvement with Innotek Australia. Everything I had done for the past 16 years, or even my entire business career, would culminate on that date, if I was successful.

My earlier discussions with business brokers and the seminars on exit strategies now paid off because I was more than ready to prepare a presentation which would put the best light on Innotek and make it attractive to RSC. I needed to focus now on their needs and how Innotek might make their company better if they were to purchase us. What benefits did we offer them that would not be available without us? I met for coffee with the professor from Bond University who had given the exit strategies seminar and outlined the opportunity to him. He agreed that it was a good opportunity and one which could be the best outcome for us. Before leaving, however, he warned me that, "You must do this deal." If I was to sell them on the benefits of having an Australian based regional office and if following that I was unable to make the sale, the potential buyer would likely open up with their own people and gradually squeeze us out. The price had to be attractive without cutting us out of value. The other benefit is that there was no agent involved and therefore no commission.

Colleen and I flew to America on June 10, heading first to Nashville for a few days at the Country Music Festival before driving over to Knoxville to meet the Radio Systems people. Nashville was hopping and was a great way to recover from jet lag and relax before our meeting the following Monday. Thanks to Keith Urban and Nicole Kidman, Australia was popular that weekend so the hospitality flowed. Also, the Socceroos were playing in the Football World Cup which was getting good coverage in American sports bars. I watched a couple of games and I was hoping for the omen of a win for Australia that weekend. Unfortunately Australia was eliminated on the Sunday and so it was that I returned to my normal scepticism regarding omens.

On Monday morning, we caught up with Titch at the office where he had arranged two days of meetings with various departments for discussions on a range of everyday matters that affected the business. The presentation to Randy Boyd and his senior management was set for Monday afternoon but no mention was made about what I would present. Maybe there had been a communications problem and they weren't really interested in my attitude toward selling. We were told of a number of new acquisitions which were either pending or active. That was encouraging.

The afternoon meeting was delayed for an hour or so which added to the tension I was feeling. For everyone else around me it was just another day but for me it was one of the biggest sales pitches of my life. At the beginning of my business career this would have been one of those very tough things, but by now I had learned to handle situations like this. Once the meeting started and I had the floor I was very comfortable about the situation. I was making a presentation about a company which I loved and one which could claim to have a very successful track record. I had a great product to sell and I had an audience that was eager to buy. I was able to get the message across exactly as I had pictured it and the feedback was a roomful of interested people with the occasional nods of agreement to what I was saying. I was definitely on a high and was confident that I could not have done better. At the conclusion I asked for feedback, directing my question to Randy.

Randy looked at me and said something like, "Wow! I am blown away. I don't know what to say! We asked for an opinion about whether at some time in the future you might be interested in selling, but we never expected this." Other people in attendance all reacted with enthusiasm about the idea of having an Australian regional office. Questions were posed for follow up and the process by which RSC evaluated acquisitions was explained—all good buying signals. The meeting concluded with a promise to get back to me after the proposal was discussed at the next meeting of their acquisitions team and subsequent consideration by their board.

I came out of that meeting confident that we had taken the process to the next stage and that it would lead to the sale of Innotek to Radio Systems. That evening we dined with Randy and his wife, further cementing the positive feeling I had about the earlier meeting. Titch confessed his surprise at the full-on sales presentation I had made about "my interest in selling." I could not understand what the fuss was about. My opinion was, if you are interested in selling, then sell! It goes to show that often the best way of communicating is to be up front, laying your cards on the table and making sure that people understand where you are coming from. Radio Systems would now be in no doubt that I was interested in selling and furthermore what price we were expecting to achieve. The next move was theirs.

After two days at Knoxville it was time to move on and start our holidays. It was almost surreal to be winding down for a holiday after the high of my selling activity. There was no sense in worrying about it. It would be at least a couple of months before any feedback would be forthcoming from Radio Systems and there was nothing further that I could do in the meantime. So we just went ahead and had a great holiday. Canada, England and France were all very beautiful and it was most enjoyable to catch up with family and friends, but the possibility of a business deal was never far from my mind.

As it turned out, the wait was about as expected because, on August 26, I received an email from Radio Systems with proposed contract of sale documentation for a settlement completion date of January 1, 2011. The price offered and the formula for including any profit we made up to the completion date was less than our valuation of the company but the simplicity of the transaction and the fact that I would get full pay-out at completion was attractive. I would be required to work for the company until December 31, 2011 as Managing Director and all business would initially continue without change. We accepted the offer and Innotek Australia was as good as sold.

I asked Paul Everingham to act for us and since Radio Systems did not have any legal representation in Australia, Paul was asked to prepare a draft agreement. Although Paul was very ethical in drafting an agreement to suit both parties, it was still an advantage to have him draw up the agreement. Radio Systems had been quite clear in their offer and Paul's agreement reflected that clarity, but legal agreements can complicate and cause difficulties in a sale such as this. As with the RSPCA case, I believed it to be important to have good legal advice and this was borne out before the deal was completed.

There were some delays to the completion of the sale, mostly due to the fact that Radio Systems were going through other acquisitions at the same time. The deal was finally completed a month late on January 31, so from February 1st, I was once more an employee, at least until the end of that year. Colleen decided not to continue working and retired as of that date.

Paul Everingham's comments about the sale were interesting. He said that RSC must have had a lot of trust in me to be willing to structure almost all the payment up front and only hold back a small adjustment to reflect the changes taking place in the on-going business. In his view, most company sales like this have a significant proportion of the purchase price held back and his advice was to consider the real purchase price as the up-front payment and to consider the performance component as the gravy, because it was often not paid.

I still owned our other company, Orion Solar, and we had agreed with Radio Systems that I would be spending as much as twenty per cent of my time with that company for the remainder of 2011. As to the future, what would I do with my time? Richard was running Orion but I was sure there would be an opportunity to keep my hand in there. Thus, I still had that company as a possible future challenge, should I become overwhelmed by the reality of retirement.

CHAPTER 23

※

LOOKING BACK

As I hike up the highlands, toward the plateau of retirement, it seems a good time to review my successful and not-so-successful ventures. Innotek Australia has certainly been the most successful venture, although Orion Solar continues to grow and could take its place in the sun, in the future. I have ended up comfortably well off and financially independent, and that was one of my original goals. I suppose luck has played a part in making Innotek a success, but perhaps all the other companies I created were simply practice for this one. I think it does indicate that an entrepreneur should keep trying and never give up.

The monetary gain is great, and it would be a worry if it wasn't there, but I don't think this has been the biggest reward. All of it has been a lot of fun. I have enjoyed building businesses and I think the challenge of doing so is an art as much as a science. Not only that, I have worked with some real characters along the way. My colleagues at IBM were great people but, after meeting some of them in their retirement years, I got a glimpse of what I might have been, had I not taken a stab at the unknown and hitched myself to the entrepreneurship star. It is a very reassuring glimpse.

All of my ventures have revolved around the introduction of a new product or service. The Diffusion of Innovations theory comes to mind. The adoption of new products or services by the public—the marketplace—follows a curve, over time, but its shape and progress are hard to predict. Certain innovations quickly catch on with the public and the curve of product acceptance rises rapidly, then falls away to almost nothing. Such products or services are known as fads—the Hula Hoop, the Pet Rock, the Lambada. Other innovations, like casual clothes made from blue denim, Coca Cola, or small, fuel-efficient cars, diffuse more slowly within markets, but have extremely long product lives. Most new products and services fall somewhere between these extremes. The first users are the innovators, the brave souls of the marketplace, the risk-takers. They are often the opinion leaders. They tell others about their experiences with the innovation. If these are positive and the innovators are persuasive, they are followed in the marketplace by the early-adopters. If the innovation continues to be useful—and talked about, promoted, and widely distributed—the, so called, early-majority become users, and the innovation approaches peak sales or peak acceptance in people's lives. Finally, when the innovation's usefulness is undeniable and overwhelming, the remainder of the market adopts it—the late-majority, as they are called—and then, last of all, the die-hard, over-cautious, conservative group, known as the laggards. By then, just about everybody in the marketplace has tried and adopted the innovation. But the problem is this: it is very difficult for the company taking on the product development, commercialisation and marketing of the innovation to influence the diffusion curve. So much depends on whether, and how quickly, users of the innovation communicate their results with it, how slowly or quickly its benefits and usefulness become known in the potential market, and its availability in the market.

Most of my companies introduced products and services that had to appeal to the innovators and early adopters of the marketplace, before the acceptance curve could climb to greater sales and broader market penetration. Taking Innotek as an example, in 1995, the idea of placing an electronic collar on a dog to control its behaviour was something only the innovators in the pet market would try. By the year 2000, word was spreading—and it was positive—so the early-adopters became Innotek customers. It was probably not until 2005, or later, that the early-majority took up the product and they are still our market's driving force, at the time of writing. As a market innovation in Australia, it is almost certain that the negative portrayal of our electronic collar by the Royal Society for the Prevention of Cruelty to Animals slowed down its acceptance and delayed the progress of the adoption curve.

Comma Services, Integrant Services, Micos Computer Systems, WordPro, Orion International, Orion Systems, Innotek Australia and Orion Solar all fit into the type of business that has an innovation to offer and needs to nurture its progress through the diffusion curve of market acceptance and adoption. And this has always taken longer than I originally anticipated. In other words, I had always been overconfident about how quickly I would succeed. I had to learn to be persistent and to find ways of stretching out my investment capital, in order to survive until the business did take off.

Sometimes, it is necessary to adjust the business plan to the pace of market acceptance and this usually means finding more capital to bridge the gap. Comma Services found a venture capital company to pump in the funds during the delay in market development. Some of my other ventures showed that starting a business under the wing of another one was a very successful way around this. For example, Innotek was started while Orion Systems was still bringing in revenue and profits, and Orion Solar was established as a division within Innotek, before it stood on its own.

The other problem with pioneering a new product or service is that there are no published data showing what might be achievable with a given business, and no yardsticks to measure one's success. People would often ask me what market share my business had and I couldn't answer, because there were no data on the size of the market for the product or service I was offering. Similarly, we often could not identify our competitors because we were offering a unique product or service. Thus, we sometimes took the big-picture view. For example, Innotek offered a method of keeping a dog securely enclosed on its property, using an electronic containment system. In that case, our competitors would be the suppliers of traditional fencing and dog runs. But what size was the overall market for these differing solutions? It is very difficult to know.

By contrast, if you were starting up, say, an electrical goods retail store, there would be an abundance of information on the performance of electrical goods stores for a specific country, against which one could plan and measure a new business. Furthermore, one could visit competing stores in order to gauge what they did well and use this information to improve one's competitiveness. So, the challenge of launching a new business is one thing, whereas starting a new business which is introducing a new product or service, is quite another. Perhaps this is what sets apart an entrepreneur from the average businessman.

One of the key factors in building any business is to find and recruit talented employees. I have made mistakes along the way, but my successful hires have outnumbered the duds and were instrumental in achieving what I did. A recent survey by an international recruiting firm in Australia found that almost half of new hires were duds. The cost of employing the wrong individual can be enormous, not just in lost productivity but also in staff morale, as well as the wasted resources in order to replace the individual through further recruitment. Potential candidates, like new business opportunities, are frequently revealed in subtle ways. One needs to be receptive to this fact and take advantage of such opportunities when they arise. Use traditional recruiting techniques, by all means, but be prepared to look outside the square to find the real stars.

I have always tried to give my employees the freedom to grow and develop. One of the main reasons why good people will leave a business is that they feel they are no longer growing in the job. The downside in encouraging employees to develop is that they might grow so fast that you can't keep up with them and they leave for even greener pastures. There's no sense in worrying about this because, eventually, you would probably lose this person anyway. But if you don't encourage your people to develop, then your business growth will stall too. I retain a bit of pride in having helped someone achieve new heights as a result of working with me, however small my contribution might have been. In one such instance, I helped start the career of someone selling our MICOS systems who went on to become a Vice President of Intel Corporation.

Another lesson I have learned, in building a business that markets a product from North America, is the need to keep investing time and effort to ensure that the supplier is always on side. Besides wanting the best pricing and credit terms from the supplier, it is important to be seen by the supplier as the very best team member they could have in your part of the world. The need for this kind of effort was forever evident in the relationships with Epic Data, Innotek Inc., Carmanah, and Radio Systems. There is a tendency among North American companies to conclude that the best way to operate overseas, especially in English-speaking countries, is to treat the local representative like a domestic branch office. The reasoning is that, "If it works in Houston, Seattle or Montreal, then it must work in Australia." The reality is quite different and the business culture, regulatory environment, and market conditions in the overseas arena are often disturbingly baffling, if not shockingly alien.

The frustrating part of this problem is that there is usually a much larger team on the North American supplier's home ground and many of those team members have to be educated about the impact of their decisions on the Australian market.

There will continually be people back at the supplier's office saying, "Why do they do it that way? We could do much better with a company that operates like they do in Houston." Part of the reason why Orion Systems ceased to do business with Epic Data was a decision by a manager in Vancouver to take over a contract which Orion Systems was signing with Australia Post. He believed that Epic Data should deal directly with Australia Post because Epic Data had a better chance of fulfilling the contract. The result was that Orion Systems lost the business, Epic Data misunderstood the requirements and was unable to perform, and ended up getting sued by Australia Post for breach of contract. All this, because I had not succeeded in keeping everyone at the supplier end, on side, with the correct approach.

Every business is just a link in the supply chain and, without good suppliers and good customers working effectively together, the business will fail. It is useless to concentrate totally on getting the business if the supply end lets you down.

One major lesson from all of my businesses has been never to underestimate the importance of good systems. I am not referring to just information technology systems; I mean all systems, including the manual procedures which are put into place and documented for present and future staff to follow. It is the one thing which will give the business owner the freedom to do other things, knowing that the business will continue to function when these systems are followed. It frees the owner to invest time in planning strategies for future development and still be able to monitor the day-to-day operations. The emphasis on good systems should become a part of the organisation's culture so that employees constantly think about better ways of doing things and offer improvements for running the business.

I suppose my background in information technology helped, but I have always invested in the best IT systems that my firms could afford. With the changes that have taken place in IT technology, over the span of my business career, that means I have never stopped learning. In my companies, we have gone from one-write systems, to batch computing, to multi-user systems, to PCs and now to cloud computing. Our relationship management processes have gone from hand-written diaries, to CRM systems accessible anywhere around the globe, even via a mobile phone. Communication processes have moved from postal services, to faxes, to emails, and Skype. Looking back, it is amazing how much change has taken place. I can remember my first photocopier, first fax, first PC and my first mobile phone. Using the latest technology suitable for our business has made a huge contribution to our success.

I am also proud that, at the end of my career, the systems being used in our business are as good as those existing anywhere. At the time of writing, the marketing of IT products and services is full of references to "cloud computing," but for us this is nothing new. Innotek Australia has been using NetSuite, a cloud computing solution, for the past six years.

So, what makes an entrepreneur? What makes a person want to start up new businesses in ways that others have not tried before? Is there a common thread that binds entrepreneurs?

I recently attended an interesting presentation at a business conference titled Understanding Entrepreneurs. The talk was given by Malcolm Gladwell, a staff writer at The New Yorker magazine and author of The Tipping Point and Outliers. One of Malcolm's key observations about entrepreneurs was their attitude toward risk. He put forward the idea that the commonly held view of entrepreneurs as being high risk takers, in a general sense, was wrong. He argued that most entrepreneurs try to avoid the usual operational risks in starting and building a business. But, he observed that most entrepreneurs are social risk takers.

Relating this to my own experience in launching a company to sell electronic collars for dogs, in my mind I was avoiding operational risk because I was sure that people would buy them. That proved to be correct and since I could buy at a low price and sell at a high price, where was the risk in that? But Malcolm was certainly onto something when it comes to social risk. Since my new business was immediately denounced by the RSPCA and the products are still considered a bit unfair to dogs, especially by those without experience in their use, I was taking a social risk. At the outset, many of our friends gave us sideways glances, indicating that they did not approve of what we were doing. So, Innotek was definitely socially risky, yet I took it on.

Orion International's business of acting as an unauthorised international lottery agent for the official Australian lotteries was completely legal, but could be viewed as something which should be outlawed or regulated. Therefore, it fits the definition of being socially risky. The fact that I had started the business in partnership with a friend who had already built a similar and successful business in Canada, showed that I had perceived the venture as being at an acceptably low operational risk.

My first business also seemed to support Malcolm's argument. Comma Services was modelled after a successful American business, so the operational risk was low. However, the social risk for myself was very high and, in fact, I promptly lost all my IBM friends as a result. Yet, I took the entrepreneurial plunge into unknown waters.

Malcolm's talk included examples of famous entrepreneurs, such as Steve Jobs. In the early years of Apple Computers, Steve Jobs visited Xerox Parc, the research and development firm in Silicon Valley which had developed the graphic user interface (GUI), the mouse, and the use of screen-based icons. Steve immediately went back to Apple and ordered his engineers to drop what they were doing and to start working on a new computer, which later became the Macintosh. He saw that ordering a turnaround of his product development at Apple was operationally low-risk, while the possibility of being seen as someone who took other people's ideas was socially risky.

When asked about this later, Jobs replied, "Because we had no choice."

A similar story can be told of Bill Gates. In order to supply IBM with a suitable operating system he sourced QDOS from Tim Paterson, of Seattle Computer Products, for $50,000, keeping the IBM deal secret from Paterson. Gates saw no operational risk in the deal and, eventually, it made him a billionaire. On the other hand, it was certainly a socially risky move as he could have been seen as taking advantage of Paterson. Apparently, Tim Paterson didn't see it that way and ended up becoming an employee at Microsoft.

Malcolm Gladwell's argument that entrepreneurs are operationally risk averse, but are social risk takers, seems to have some merit. They appear to thumb their noses at convention. He further argued that Californians have a high tolerance for eccentricity, meaning that social risk-taking comes easier to them, and this might explain why entrepreneurship is so common in that state and why California is a hotbed of social change.

Another conclusion which can be drawn from the above examples is that entrepreneurs are not necessarily innovators. In none of the above examples did the entrepreneur develop the original product or service. Rather, they are the facilitators with the vision to see how the innovation can become the foundation of a successful business. By the time that vision has been translated into the launching a business venture, the entrepreneur has solved the problem of operational risk.

CHAPTER 24

NO SUNSETS

TO MARK SEVENTY YEARS of a life adventure, I celebrated a significant birthday with a dinner party for 60 friends, organised very professionally by my wonderful wife Colleen. Having travelled so much during those years, I have left behind many friends in various parts of the world. But for that fact, the party would have been considerably larger. Colleen had stitched together a photographic memento of my life, projected on the wall of the hall where the party took place, on Mount Tamborine—at the edge of the Gold Coast Hinterland. The guests were mostly local friends from my business and social life, but some had travelled from the United Kingdom, Canada and other parts of Australia to be there. It made me realise how lucky I am. One special guest was Barry de Ferranti who was responsible for my move from Canada to Australia, was a guest at our wedding and was present at the ceremony when we became Australian citizens

I certainly don't feel as though I have finished striving for new opportunities and I am sure there are some new ventures out there, waiting for me. I have a few regrets about the decisions I have made along the way, but I consider regret to be quite a normal emotion. Reviewing the way things happened and feeling remorseful about the way a situation was handled creates a way to improve one's response should a similar thing reoccur.

The big message that runs through my mind, over and over again, is that life is too short. I was a slow starter in life and I was thirty years old before I had a realistic view of what I could accomplish. Should I have gone out, on my own, earlier? Possibly, but that would have diminished the value I gained from serving in the Royal Air Force, or working for IBM in the UK and Canada. My business experience at Comma and Micos in Canada were fast-moving times, so there was not much opportunity to have made more out of those years. They were the years when I learned more about business, at a faster rate than at any other time in my life. They were also years when I learned, to my detriment, to be more cautious about business deals and the ambitions of people whose goals did not necessarily align with mine—all good lessons, even though the cost was the loss of a company. But it was better to have made that mistake before I turned 40, rather than after I had reached 60.

There were times when I could have accomplished more in Australia, but the trade-off was lifestyle. During the Orion Systems years, it would have been the right business decision to move to Sydney, but I chose to stay on the Gold Coast because that's where I loved to be. Had I relocated, Orion Systems would have evolved into a different business and I would have avoided flogging a dead horse with the obsolete Epic Data product line. But I had seen too many Sydney business people working toward the goal of retiring on the Gold Coast; I was already living there.

Building a business is part science and part art. I have looked at my companies as an artist might look at a painting. There is great joy in seeing a business slowly develop toward the vision that was formed in one's mind when the idea was first conceived. Taking the analogy further, in my case the business created was the work of an Impressionist, rather than that of a realist. I have had some unconventional businesses. Of course, there were also those businesses which failed to develop as per the original vision, but I tended to put those out of my mind and move on to a new vision.

Another reward I value highly is the satisfaction of having helped someone move ahead in life, no matter how small a part I had played in that role. I know this does not apply solely to the entrepreneur, but it is something I look back upon with a sense of fulfilment. Having been told that I was a good mentor to a few of my employees is one of the things I am most proud of.

Whoever coined the phrase, "The school of hard knocks" accurately described the actual training course that comes with starting and running a business. The learning may not be as structured as that offered by "The College of Knowledge" in obtaining a degree and a certificate of completion, but the hard-knocks skills of actual experience are invaluable. In my own case, the Australian Institute of Management recognised my experience and accepted me as a member, which allows me to put the letters AAIM after my name. If letters are what matters to a person, certainly there are easier ways to obtain them. But the entrepreneurial experience is an education in itself.

Finally, the goal of an entrepreneur must be to build wealth. Becoming rich may not be the actual target, but the motivation of ending up better off than you would, as an employee, is a strong one. In my case, I have spent many years making less than I would, as an employee, and I have risked all of our assets on many occasions. What would be the sense in this, if it did not create the opportunity for ample financial independence in the long run? In our case, my wife and I devised an exit plan to achieve a comfortable retirement, with the possibility of more wealth-building if existing and future investments are successful.

For me, a great benefit of starting and building new businesses is the large number of interesting and inspiring characters that I got to know along the way. I can see, now, that I would never have met such a cast of characters had I stayed an employee of IBM, or some other big organisation. In recent years, with the help of the

Internet, I have been able to reconnect with some of the people from my years as an employee, and later as a businessman. When traveling to Canada and the USA I have caught up with many friends and work associates from IBM, Kinsmen, and from my days at Micos. Some former colleagues have also moved on to new locations but I exchange emails with such friends in Europe, the USA and Mexico. At times, my contact attempts are tinged with sadness; a reply to one of my emails informed me that my good friend, and Orion International partner, Ernest Priess, had died. He was one of the most imaginative entrepreneurs I have encountered.

My family members have always been supportive of my ideas and adventures, and what a delightful outcome it is for an English-born entrepreneur, oozing with wanderlust, to have them all living in close proximity to me! At age 44, Wales-born son, Richard, and I are partners in Orion Solar Pty Ltd, where I still work three days a week. He and Erin will be married this year which brings the promise of more grandchildren. Alex (Alexandra, the 46-year-old, born in Chester, England) lives nearby with my grandson, Louis. And Angela, the Canadian, born in Victoria, British Columbia, is now 41 and lives with Craig about an hour's drive away, in Brisbane. My first wife, May, is 71 and lives close by in the suburb of Mudgeeraba. The costs, to them, of my travels and tribulations have been temporary and I feel proud that they've become established in their own right, while the family unit has remained intact.

Would I relive the adventure of being a global entrepreneur? If only I could get a second chance!

What of the future? Writing this book has kindled a desire to write about a far greater person than I am. My ancestor, Walter Henry Medhurst, who started the Parapattan Orphanage, in Jakarta, is a man who spent his entire life following his belief that he could make a difference in the world. His achievements are extraordinary. He was among the first missionaries to China, being on a team of four people who translated the Bible into Chinese, and serving on the first Shanghai District Council. His recognition was international; the University of New York conferred on him the honorary degree of Doctor of Divinity. But for the fact that he became ill and died two days after returning home to England, he would have become better known throughout the world and probably knighted by Queen Victoria. Incredibly, there has never been a biography written about him.

There are no sunsets; this must become my very next project.

Toughing It Out

About the Author

John Holliday served in the Royal Air Force before going into the IT business in the UK, in Canada and then Australia. A visit to a still-functioning orphanage in Jakarta, founded more than 180 years before by his missionary ancestor, Walter Medhurst, kindled his interest in recording Walter's life. So became 'Mission to China: How an Englishman Brought the West to the Orient', published first in England followed by a Chinese version published in Taiwan.

During the research into Walter Medhurst's life, John uncovered the extraordinary life of Clara Colby, whose grandmother was Walter Medhurst's sister. Clara Colby, he determined, must be the subject of my next book.

John lives with his wife, Colleen, on the Gold Coast in Queensland, Australia.

www.ingramcontent.com/pod-product-compliance
Lightning Source LLC
Chambersburg PA
CBHW010245010526
44107CB00063B/2688